KT-179-752

Circle Time for the
Very Young

A Lucky Duck Book

226 065

Circle Time for the Very Young

Second edition

Margaret Collins

P·C·P

Paul Chapman
Publishing

© Margaret Collins 2007

First published 2007

Apart from any fair dealing for the purposes of research or private study, or criticism or review, as permitted under the Copyright, Designs and Patents Act, 1988, this publication may be reproduced, stored or transmitted in any form, or by any means, only with the prior permission in writing of the publishers, or in the case of reprographic reproduction, in accordance with the terms of licences issued by the Copyright Licensing Agency. Enquiries concerning reproduction outside those terms should be sent to the publishers.

Rights to copy pages marked as handouts, certificates or overhead foils are extended to the purchaser of the publication for his/her use.

The right of the Author to be indentified as Author of this work has been asserted by him/her in accordance with the Copyright, Design and Patents Act 1988.

 Paul Chapman Publishing
A SAGE Publications Company
1 Oliver's Yard
55 City Road
London EC1Y 1SP

SAGE Publications Inc.
2455 Teller Road
Thousand Oaks, California 91320

SAGE Publications India Pvt Ltd
B 1/I 1 Mohan Cooperative Industrial Area
Mathura Road, New Delhi 110 044

SAGE Publications Asia-Pacific Pte Ltd
33 Pekin Street #02-01
Far East Square
Singapore 048763

www.luckyduck.co.uk

Illustrations by: Philippa Drakeford

Library of Congress Control Number: 2006938970

British Library Cataloguing in Publication data

A catalogue record for this book is available from the British Library

ISBN 978-1-4129-3030-7

Typeset by C&M Digitals (P) Ltd, Chennai, India
Printed in Great Britain by The Cromwell Press, Trowbridge, Wiltshire
Printed on paper from sustainable resources

Contents

NORWICH CITY COLLEGE LIBRARY

Stock No.   226065

Class   372. 241 COL

Cat.   Proc.

Acknowledgements

- Noreen Wetton, a valued friend and colleague from whom I learned so much but who sadly died in January 2006.
- Colleagues and friends at the Health Education Unit of the School of Education, University of Southampton.
- Philippa Drakeford for her charming drawings.
- Jake French, Orchard Infant School, Southampton, for the cover drawing.

Introduction

Circle Time cannot better be described than in the words of Dr John Thacker, University of Exeter, writing the foreword for a book about Circle Time.[1]

> Circle Time is an approach which aims to mobilise the power of the group experience for the benefit of the individual children in class ... where everyone is equal, everybody can be seen and heard, people can make eye contact, they can speak to one another more easily, there are no barriers such as tables or desks and everyone feels part of the group.

Circle Time is a structured, regular occasion when a class group meets in a circle to speak, listen, interact and share concerns. The circle is a symbol of unity and co-operation, indicating that the group is working together to support one another and to take equal responsibility for addressing issues.

Circle Time helps children to understand and value themselves and others as well as forming positive relationships. It can enhance children's confidence and self-esteem in providing a safe environment where they can explore feelings, talk about concerns and express opinions, with each child having the opportunity to speak and to be listened to. This enables communication and respect for others to occur naturally and helps children to practise the conversational skills of listening, answering and waiting their turn to contribute. Children need to become skilled in the use of language to be able to talk about and deal with their emotions and feelings and this means a lot of talking and listening. It is all too easy to 'talk to' young children and to think that they are absorbing what we say; only by giving them a chance to express themselves verbally can we enhance their language skills, helping them to absorb the words they need in order to talk about and manage feelings and emotions.

Circle Time is the perfect venue for extending emotional literacy skills, knowledge, attitudes and values in Personal, Social, Health and Emotional Education (PSHE) and citizenship. Circle Time gives children the opportunity of participating in discussion, allowing them to agree or to disagree with points that others make. It can be a platform for each child to be himself and say what he wishes and to know that he will be listened to with respect. As part of citizenship, children are taught to take part in discussions with the whole class, to take part in simple debates on topical issues, to recognise what they like and dislike and to respect the opinions of others; Circle Time will allow for all this. Through discussion children will learn to look at alternatives and resolve differences. Given the opportunity, they will learn to recognise and name their feelings and learn to deal with them in a positive way. In Circle Time children will agree to and follow rules for their group and classroom and come to understand how rules help us all.

However, Circle Time is not an education strategy in itself – it is not only the quality of the work done within Circle Time that makes it a useful way of communicating with children; it is in setting the context before, and using discussion after, that can make Circle Time a truly productive tool to use with young children. Circle Time must:

[1]Curry, M. and Bromfield, C. (1994) *Personal and Social Education for Primary Schools Through Circle Time*, Nasen Enterprises Ltd, Stafford.

- be planned, as with any other teaching
- have specified learning objectives
- be part of a progressive programme
- be evaluated.

Most books about Circle Time are for older primary pupils and do not take sufficient account of the social and language skills of younger pupils. This book is different as it focuses on the early years.

Circle Time needs to be a regular occurrence – at least once a week. For younger children a short session of 10–15 minutes a day may be best; with older juniors a session lasting 30–40 minutes a week may be better.

It takes quite a lot of skill to run Circle Time effectively with young children if real learning is to take place. Time taken in the early stages to establish the format and organisation of Circle Time is not wasted and will pay dividends in future sessions. Those who experience difficulties may need to shorten the session or look carefully at the content. Make it lively and fun and children will respond well and look forward to Circle Time.

Schools develop Circle Time in their own way. The following framework provides guidelines which are meant to be used flexibly. Schools which have a well-developed ethos of Circle Time could add to this framework.

Overall framework for Circle Time

Rules for Circle Time

It is important to set rules for Circle Time, so that everyone knows the conditions and can abide by them. You may like the children to set the rules themselves, once you have explained the format for and purpose of Circle Time. Rules can be as simple as:

- only one person talks at a time
- listen and look at the person who is talking
- don't touch the people sitting next to you
- don't say things that would upset people
- 'pass' if you need time to think – there will be another opportunity to say what you wish at the end.

What size of circle?

As the children mature, and once the format of Circle Time has been established, their improved skills and experience will enable them to respond in larger groups and circles. Until this time children will respond much better in very small groups.

This book concentrates on simple activities that can be done by the youngest children in small groups. Most Circle Time books suggest a large circle, but this is not appropriate for very young children who find it easy to tell but hard to listen. It is important that small, easily managed groups give plenty of opportunity for all children to take an active part and have their say.

Forming the circle

While older children will soon learn how to form their circle of chairs in a sensible and safe way, younger children in school will find it easier to form their circle by standing and holding hands before sitting down in that circle. You may like to use carpet squares for younger children; this has the advantage not only of comfort and warmth, but gives children a set boundary for their sitting space. Some teachers are happy to sit on the floor, but if not, their chair(s) should be low. Teachers will need to make sure that the same children do not always sit by them, perhaps by choosing their place after the circle is formed. All adults in the class should join the circle; its power is diminished if other adults are busily working on other things outside the circle.

Signals

You will need to use signals for quiet at the start of Circle Time and after a noisy activity. You may already have signals in place as part of the class routine. Some teachers sing and clap to a musical 'Are you ready?' and the children answer 'Yes we are'. Others use a bell or gong as a starting signal or a notice with 'Please be quiet' on one side and 'Thank you' on the other. Some raise a hand and train the children to copy this action.

You may like to select some object to pass around the circle as tangible evidence of the right to speak. Tell the children that this is what people used to do in the olden days when the Elders of the village had their meetings. Choose a special object only for this purpose – a baton, a large shell – or use an appropriate object according to the content of Circle Time.

A regular structure

A regular structure for each session is desirable. The following will give you some ideas as to how to develop a framework for each session:

- Welcome – go around the circle saying hello to each child by name.
- Teacher time – set the theme of the session, mention birthdays, special occasions, achievements.
- Children time – ask the children if there is anything they want to tell. You may want to limit this to five different children each day, so as to use Circle Time effectively.
- Main theme of the session.
- Songs, games, or fun endings.

Inclusion techniques

It is important to keep Circle Time alive and active. There are various strategies you can use to do this, for example:

- **Change places** – when a child repeats a word or phrase that has already been said by another child ask the second child to change places with the child who last said it.

- **Hands-up session** – an opportunity for children to offer ideas by raising their hands, i.e. not going round the circle or group.

- **Imagine it** – close your eyes and make a picture in your head of the situation described.

- **Jot down** – have a notebook or piece of paper with you and jot down some of the appropriate words and phrases the children offer you. You can discuss these with the children after the activity, rather than break the flow at the time. You may be able to use these words later in the session.

- **Share ideas** – divide the children into groups and give them a topic to explore. Allow the groups to have a few minutes to share ideas and then come together in a circle again. Larger groups may be more appropriate for older children.

- **Tell a story** – read the story provided to the children and ask them to think about what they have heard. Alternatively, divide the children into groups and ask them to compose a story on the topic. Come together in a circle and invite volunteers from each group to tell their story. Discuss each story after it has been told.

- **Pass the face** – say 'How does your face look when you are angry?' The first child makes an appropriate face, then shows it to the next person, who turns to show their appropriate face to the next person to them.

- **Pass the sentence** – start a sentence and ask the nearest child to finish it and pass it on; for example, 'I feel happy when …' (Allow children to 'pass'.)

- **Question and answer** – e.g. tell the nearest child who you are and ask him who he is, for example 'I am Mrs Jones, who are you?' The child replies 'I am John'. John turns from you and says to the nearest child – 'I am John, who are you?'

- **Stand and tell** – ask volunteers to stand and talk about your topic; standing gives confidence and allows others to focus on the speaker.

- **Stand and show** – children sitting with pictures or work individually stand up to show and talk about their work and sit down before another child stands.

- **Stand up if** … – ask the children to stand up if they agree/disagree with a suggestion or to show a particular point of view, e.g. 'Stand up if you have one brother', 'Stand up if making your friend happy was hard to do'.

- **Stand and mime** – children, individually or several at a time, mime an activity or skill at the front (or in the middle of the circle) and those watching try to guess what they are doing. The child miming might be asked to select children to guess the mime until someone gives the correct answer.

- **Stand, count and sit down quickly** – this helps to find out numbers of children who gave various responses. All children stand. Ask those who gave a certain response to raise a hand, then count themselves, you write down the number and only these children sit down. Ask children who gave a different response to raise a hand and so on.

- **Stand, tell and sit down quickly** – ask the children a question that has a yes or no answer. Tell them to stand, say 'yes' or 'no', and sit down quickly. This creates a wave effect.

- **Touch your** … – ask children to touch their nose, shoulders, ears, etc. depending on whether they agree or don't agree, for example 'If you have a sister, touch your nose', 'If you have two sisters, touch your ears', 'If you have a brother, raise your shoulders'.

- **Vote with your feet** – offer various places in the classroom for children to stand according to which choice they make. Ask them to stand in a line in that place and count themselves. The first child says 'one', the second says 'two' and so on. Note the number of responses for each choice.

PSHE in Circle Time

It is important to make sure that the content of Circle Time is interesting and fun but also educational. Circle Time is a particularly useful tool for PSHE as well as citizenship. Use the theme part of the session as an opener by asking children to finish such sentences as 'I show I am a good friend when I ...', 'When people shout at me I feel ...', 'I like growing up because I can ...', 'I keep safe on the roads when I ...'

Use Circle Time as a starting point for projects or centres of interest and as a way of finding out what children themselves know about the subject and what they bring with them.

Circle Time activities reinforce the importance of turn-taking and sharing the adult's time while at the same time allowing each child to partake in an activity. The activities in this book provide the foundation for PSHE on which the later curriculum rests.

In Circle Time young children have the opportunity to:

- listen to others
- be listened to
- talk to the whole group
- improve their social skills
- co-operate with children and adults
- increase their self-confidence
- improve their self-esteem
- get to know their classmates
- improve their friendship-making skills
- identify and voice their own needs
- become aware of the needs of others
- realise that their problems are often common to the group and can be solved.

Listening skills

Right from the start, and with all children, explain that when someone is talking it is everyone's job to really listen. Children will need to learn the skill of really listening – this involves looking at the person talking – looking at their eyes or their mouth.

Make up some games to improve this skill – such as:

- speak without sound and ask the children to tell you what they think your lips have said
- use facial expressions to show how you are feeling and ask the children to tell you
- play 'Chinese Whispers' with a small group in the middle of the circle or group (e.g. with no more than five children in a line, whisper a short phrase which the child will repeat to the next person, who repeats to the next and so on until the last child speaks it out loud. Then the teacher says out loud what the first whisper has been).

Insist that the children look at the child or adult talking, making sure the children don't comment or interrupt until that person has finished.

Children will need help to learn to concentrate and think about what the person means when they are talking.

Only permit the next speaker to talk when they have used your recognised signal – a raised hand, a raised finger, or whatever signal is used.

Explain to children that we can tell when they are really listening, by the way they look. The adult can demonstrate this by their own and other children's body language – nodding, smiling, frowning, showing empathy.

These skills do not come easily to young children, but Circle Time is an ideal opportunity for children to learn the skill of effective listening.

Co-operation

Circle Time can only operate well if all the children co-operate and engage in appropriate behaviour. There will be children who find it difficult to concentrate or who distract other children. There are various ways to deal with this, such as:

- stop the session and remind the group of the rules
- explain that Circle Time is only possible with their concentration and co-operation
- if children are distracting others, ask them to change places with someone else, explaining why this is necessary
- be tough, but only ever exclude children from the group if there is some other supervised activity they can do – making sure this is not a 'treat'
- when it is necessary to give a warning, only give it once and then carry out your warning.

Organising group work

Many of the activities are arranged as small group work. One of the strengths of Circle Time activities is that children can be arranged in groups that don't follow their normal friendship or working groups. Rather than say 'get into groups of five', where children will naturally seek out their friends, it is good policy to arrange the groups so as to get children to work with all the children in the class at various times. You can do this by asking the children to number themselves, one to ten repeatedly around the circle, and then by asking all the 'ones' to work in a group and so on. You could use the mixing-up games ideas, below.

Mixing-up games

Mixing-up games also give all the children a chance to work with others in the class. Go around the circle and give each child a designation, such as:

Train, boat, plane (transport)

Apple, cherry, banana, strawberry, plum (fruits)

Lion, cat, dog, rabbit (animals).

At any time you can say: 'Trains change places' or 'Lions change places'. If you say 'Animals [or transport or fruit] change places', everyone will stand up and change places.

What you get in this book

This book has been developed to help you plan and carry out Circle Time for the youngest children in school. It provides separate activities for:

- Nursery, Reception children – on the left-hand page, headed 'younger children'.
- Key Stage 1 or younger Key Stage 2 children – on the right-hand page, headed 'older children'.

Younger children (3–6 years)

For the youngest children it is essential to start with a small group of no more than ten children. Initially gather them together in a small, intimate group sitting round your feet. A circle – even a small circle – is difficult to maintain for very young children and has that large, threatening open space between you and them. A group gives security to the youngest children; as they mature and become more secure in knowing the routine of Circle Time, the group can be enlarged and finally a circular arrangement will be successful.

In nurseries or pre-schools where the organisation is of three groups of ten children it is best to have Circle Time in three groups, each controlled by the adult in charge of that group. These three groups could be sited in areas of the nursery where it is quiet enough not to be overheard or influenced by the other groups and could take place at the same time. If not, it might be more satisfying to have each group's Circle Time in the quiet area at different times of the day. Even with many 'rising fives' Circle Time will still work better with small numbers – perhaps half the class at a time.

Start by having short sessions of 10 or 15 minutes until the children are used to the situation. Follow a regular pattern, so that these young children know what to expect. Always start with:

- a welcome
- then teacher's time
- followed by children's time
- the main theme
- and an ending activity.

Making the circle for younger children

Young children may find that work in an open circle is not comfortable and even worrying, being used to making a close group around the teacher for their together times. Circle Time activities fit well into this close-knit formation and teachers may find that this arrangement is easier to handle than a huge, open circle.

Where teachers of Nursery or Reception children want to try an open circle it should be small – small enough to allow everyone to take turns without getting bored – perhaps only five or six children, certainly no more than ten. Some books on Circle Time suggest using carpet squares – one for each child – and these will help the children to stay in one place. Some books also suggest using chairs for sitting. This is not really appropriate for the youngest children as it could take up far too much time to organise at both ends of the sessions.

Older children (6–9 years)

Older children still need close contact with their teacher, but most will now respond well in larger groups. At six years old the whole class sitting in a group around you will work quite well. At seven an open circle might be possible – but much depends on the stage of the children.

If children are to sit still for the whole of the Circle Time, consider carefully the length of time for each session. Young children quickly get bored if they are expected to sit still for long – better to have two short Circle Times of 15 minutes each than one of half an hour which doesn't work.

Longer sessions will work if you have a moving game or activity which allows children to move about, change places or go off to work in pairs or small groups. This will engage all the pupils' interest, give an opportunity for them to move and allow Circle Time to run for longer than in more static sessions.

With young KS1 pupils aged five or six, whole-class work is preferable, but could be difficult to maintain in an open circle unless the children are particularly mature and can relate to you in this open space. You may still find that a fairly tight group instead of a circle is more easily organised and managed.

Making the circle for older children

With KS1 children, not yet ready for a circle, you might find it useful to try two circles, one inside the other. It is certainly easier to manage the activities (and not miss anyone out) in a circular formation and this allows children to be closer to the teacher than if they were in one huge circle. Initially organise this by making one circle with children from half the class. When this group is settled and sitting, ask the other half of the class to make another circle outside the first and sit with them there.

With older KS2 children, more ready for an open circle, ask the children to hold hands before sitting on the floor in the space they have made. In this way the children will usually be sitting by a friend and will feel comfortable in the circle.

To form one large, open circle with older children may mean organising furniture. This is quite possible with older children and does not take too much time as long as you give explicit instructions so that they know exactly what you want them to do. Try Circle Time outside on the grass in the summer.

It is useful to start each session by reminding the children of the rules; you could have these written up nearby. Before each session you could read them or ask for a reading volunteer to read them.

Haiku (pronounced 'high-koo', plural the same)

Haiku are very short poems; the Haiku Society of America (www.hsa-haiku.org) has called haiku 'poem[s] in which Nature is linked to human nature'.

Using haiku and asking children to compose some sits comfortably with PSHE and citizenship. It can be organised and reviewed in Circle Time.

The following haiku by Eric Finney,[1] born in 1929, sums up the definition beautifully.

There are several books about haiku in libraries, for example *The Haiku Anthology*, edited by Cor Van den Heuvel (W.W. Norton & Co., 2000).

> Poem in three lines
>
> Five syllables, then seven
>
> Five again. No rhyme.

Each topic explored here contains a haiku for the children to consider; in each section children are asked to suggest words to use in a relevant haiku which can be composed by the teacher and children or by older children on their own.

Resources

The book concludes with a list of children's picture books which are very suitable for discussion on various PSHE topics, as well as a list of songbooks to enhance Circle Time and other books about Circle Time.

[1]from a poster, Pictorial Charts Educational Trust 1995, 27 Kirchen Road, London W13 0UD.

Framework for Circle Time

It is important to create a regular format for the sessions – it helps to organise time and gives children a routine to expect.

1. Welcome

Start by saying hello to each child by name with each child replying.

2. Teacher time

If there is anything special to say such as recognising a child's birthday or remarking on something, this is the time to do it. Keep this short.

3. Children time

Ask the children if there is anything they want to tell. By giving the shell or object to each child who is speaking, it preserves the right for that child to speak. You may need to limit the number of children who can hold the floor – say five each session. Other children can come later and tell on their own or wait until the next Circle Time.

4. Themes

There are eight main PSHE themes in this book:

1. Friends and friendships
2. Growing and growing up
3. Keeping safe
4. Self-esteem
5. Keeping healthy
6. Feelings and persuasion
7. Citizenship
8. Loss, grief and separation.

These themes are subdivided into six or eight topics, each having two sections on facing pages, one for younger children and one for older children. Each topic has suggestions for further work which often includes ideas for a display of children's work.

The activities for both younger and older children are interchangeable and can be used to suit the abilities and skills of the children you work with – you can mix and match them. Teachers of children with special needs or those in special schools can find the appropriate level for their pupils.

5. Songs, games, or various fun endings

Most teachers have a repertoire of songs, poems, games and ring games. This is a relaxing way to end each session. With younger children use nursery rhymes or counting games – e.g. 'Five brown buns' (traditional), 'One elephant' (Okki Tokki Unga). There is a list of songbooks for young children at the end of this book.

The eight PSHE themes

These activities are intended to be slotted into Circle Time after 'Children's time' and before your fun ending.

Theme 1 Friends and friendships

1. Who I am
2. What is a friend?
3. Being a good friend
4. New friends, old friends
5. Quarrels
6. Making up
7. Making others happy
8 When friends move – separation.

Theme 2 Growing and growing up

1. When I was very young
2. Now I am ... I can ...
3 Looking back
4. It takes time to grow
5. I know I'm getting bigger because ...
6. Who helps us to grow and learn?
7. New responsibilities
8. Looking forward.

Theme 3 Keeping safe

1. Who am I?
2. Who keeps me safe?
3. I can keep myself safe
4. At home
5. Outside
6. Keeping my body healthy and safe
7. People I need to keep safe from
8. Our messages about keeping safe.

Theme 4 Self-esteem

1. Names are important
2. Everyone is special
3. Body language
4. What I'm good at
5. Empathy
6. Working together.

Theme 5 Keeping healthy

1. A happy, healthy person
2. We need to exercise
3. Sleep and rest
4. Keeping clean
5. Healthy eating
6. Emotional health.

Theme 6 Feelings and persuasion

1. Feeling good
2. Feelings we share
3. How can we tell how people are feeling?
4. Feelings change
5. Feeling afraid – what can we do?
6. Good persuasion
7. Bad persuasion
8. Saying 'no' to bad persuasion.

Theme 7 Citizenship

1. Why do we need rules?
2. Rules outside school
3. Who makes the rules?
4. Other people's property and feelings
5. Being truthful
6. Losing and finding
7. Litter
8. Protecting our environment.

Theme 8 Loss, grief and separation

1. Losing something
2. Feeling sad
3. Missing someone
4. Someone's leaving
5. Changes
6. Poor Grandma.

Theme 1 Friends and friendships

1. Who I am
2. What is a friend?
3. Being a good friend
4. New friends, old friends
5. Quarrels
6. Making up
7. Making others happy
8. When friends move – separation.

We are good friends.

Explain to the children exactly what a haiku is. They don't have to abide by the 5-7-5 rule when they compose their own.

A haiku is a:
Poem in three lines
Five syllables, then seven
Five again. No rhyme.

The following haiku can be used in this section:

Who I am I know who I am, What I do and what I like, I feel good inside.	**Quarrels** Quarrels are horrid, Such a waste of time and space. Let's be friends instead.
What is a friend? A person I know, Someone I want to be with. We play together.	**Making up** It's sad to break up. It's better when you make up. Let's be friends again.
Being a good friend I'll be good to you. I'll be kind and thoughtful and Won't want my own way.	**Making others happy** What makes you happy? I'll find out how to do it. We'll always be friends.
New friends, old friends I won't forget you When a new friend comes to stay, All friends are special.	**When friends move** Moving on is hard, Don't leave me, don't go away. I won't forget you.

1. Who I am

There are many variations of this game; you can suit it to the children in your class. The main object is to be able to tell something positive about yourself and ask a friend. Here are two different questions you can use.

Question and answer

Who am I?' – tell the nearest child who you are and ask them who they are. Pass this on round the group or circle – e.g. tell the nearest child who you are and ask him who he is:

> 'I am Mrs Jones, who are you?'
> The child replies:
> 'I am John.'
> John turns from you and says to the nearest child:
> 'I am John, who are you?'

What are you good at? –

> 'I am Mrs Jones and I am good at playing tennis.
> What are you good at doing?'
> 'I am James and I am good at running. What are you good at doing?'

I like playing ball with Katie.

Touch your ...

Follow up the previous activity by asking children to touch a part of themselves if they are also good at each named activity.

Haiku

Read this haiku and talk about it. Ask the children to suggest words that they could use in a haiku. List these on the board and help the children to make them into one or more haiku. Use them and children's drawings to generate a display.

> **Who I am**
> I know who I am,
> What I do and what I like,
> I feel good inside.

Further work

Ask the children to think about what a friend of theirs likes to do. Ask the children to draw themselves with a friend, doing something their friend likes to do. Add a caption and put some of this work alongside the haiku.

1. Who I am

Ask the children to work in pairs to find out one thing about their partner. Allow only a couple of minutes for this and re-form the group or circle. (In this way children can explore what others in the class like or dislike, realising that personal preference is OK – we don't all have to like the same things.) Share what the children have discovered about their partner or friend, using the techniques below.

Pass the sentence

The first child says what their partner said they liked.

'My friend Mary likes to skate.'
'What does your friend like to do?'

The next child replies and then turns to the next person with the same question.

I have brown hair and brown eyes.
I like football.

Stand and tell – Describe yourself

Ask the children to close their eyes and think of three (more for older children) things about themselves. Ask each child to 'stand and tell' these three things. (Allow children to 'pass'.)

Haiku

Use the haiku on the facing page and talk about it. Ask the children to suggest words that they could use in a Haiku about who they are, listing these on the board. Ask the children to choose words to compose and write down their own haiku. Share these in Circle Time.

Further work

Ask each child to decorate their written haiku and display them.

Extend the display by asking them to write and draw pictures about what they like and dislike. Ask them to fold their paper in half and to draw something they like on one half and something they don't like on the other. Ask the children to think of a title – perhaps 'We don't all like the same things' or 'We are all different'.

2. What is a friend?

Ask the children to close their eyes and think of their friends and how they know that these people are their friends. Allow half a minute for this.

Pass the sentence/Jot down

Ask each child in turn to tell you one thing about a friend.

'A friend is ...'

As the children tell you, listen for any key words that tell you what a friend is and what a friend does and jot these down on paper in two lists. Allow children to 'pass' and return to these children for a second chance when everyone else has had a say. (This gives timid children more time to think.) Allow repeats.

A friend ...

plays with me
shares things
is kind
likes me
sits by me
helps me.

Touch Your . . .

Read out each list of words you have made, talk about these with the children and ask if they can add any more. Write them up somewhere. Now ask the children to help you to read their suggestions on the second list and to think of when a friend of theirs did one of these things. Go through the list, asking them to touch their chin if they have a friend who ...

Haiku

Read this haiku and talk about it. Ask the children to look again at the list of words you made and talk about those that they could use in a haiku. Help the children to make them into one or more haiku. Use them and children's drawings to generate a display.

> **What is a friend?**
> A person I know,
> Someone I want to be with.
> We play together.

Further work

Ask the children to help you to read the two word lists once each day. Children could add to each list by drawing some of the actions for you to display around the list (as clues).

Ask the children to draw a picture of themselves doing something that shows they are a good friend.

2. What is a friend?

Before you start Circle Time ask the children to draw a picture of one of their friends and to write round their picture some of the things that their friend does that show they are a friend.

Stand and show

Come together for Circle Time and ask each child to show their picture to the group and to say one of the things that their friend does. (Each child stands in turn and shows their picture to the group. Allow children to 'pass'.) Display some of these pictures under the title 'Friends and friendship'.

Jot down

Jot down the words they use about what their friend does to show they are a friend.

Pass the sentence

Go around the circle asking each child to finish this sentence in an appropriate way:

  'My friend ...'

As the children are talking make a list of what they say.

This friend is my big brother. He...

plays with me

sings to me   shares his toys

tickles me

lets me watch his video

holds my hand coming to school

At the end of the session read your list to the class and ask if they can group things on your list together in any way or put it into some kind of order.

Haiku

Use the haiku on the facing page and talk about it. Ask the children to suggest words that they could use in a haiku about friends, what they are and what they do; write these on the board. Ask the children to choose words to compose and write down their own haiku. Share these in Circle Time.

Further work

Ask the children to write out their haiku and draw a picture of some friends. Display some of them. You could make a chart of the list of words and use some of the children's pictures to decorate it. Use the words as aids to spelling or reading practice. At the next Circle Time session remind the children of the work they did.

3. Being a good friend

Ask the children to think about what being a good friend is all about.

Touch your . . .

Ask the children to touch their noses if they think they are a good friend.

Pass the sentence

'I am a good friend when I ...'

Being a good friend	
easy	**hard**
play with them	let them be first
share with them	let them choose
talk to them	listen to them
work with them.	share other friends.

Jot down

Jot down some of the key words and make a short list for everyone to see or read.

Look at what they have said and ask them if they can sort these into groups – e.g. easy to do, hard to do.

Touch your ...

Ask the children to:

- touch their elbows together if they think it's easy to be a good friend
- touch their chin if they think it's hard to be a good friend.

Ask the children to help you to count how many think it's easy.

Explain that it is sometimes hard to do what a friend wants to do if you yourself want to do something else. It gets easier if you can take turns. Can you or any of the children give examples of this?

Haiku

Read this haiku. Ask the children to look again at the list of words you made and talk about those that they could use in a haiku. Help the children to use some of these words to compose one or more haiku. Ask the children who can write to choose one to copy out and ask other children to draw pictures to illustrate them.
Use these haiku and drawings to generate a display.

> **Being a good friend**
> I'll be good to you.
> I'll be kind and thoughtful and
> Won't want my own way.

Further work

Ask the children to draw themselves being a good friend and add your writing to say what they are doing. (Children could take their pictures home to show their families or you could make a display with them.)

3. Being a good friend

Ask the children to think of a time when they did something to please a friend – perhaps something they didn't want to do, but they did it because they knew their friend wanted them to.

Pass the sentence

'I made my friend happy when I ...'

Stand up if ...

Ask the children to:

19 of us think it's easy to please a friend

10 of us think it can sometimes be hard to please a friend.

- stand up if it was hard to do that. (Count how many.)
- stand up if it was easy to do that. (Count how many.)

Pass the face

Ask the children to think of how their face looked when they were pleasing their friend and to pass this face around the group or circle – e.g. the first child makes an appropriate face, shows the next person, who turns to show their appropriate face to the next person to them.

Haiku

Use the haiku on the facing page and talk about it. Ask the children to suggest words that they could use in a haiku about being a good friend – the kinds of things they do and what they say. List these on the board. Ask the children to choose some of these or other words to compose and write down their own haiku. Share these in Circle Time. You could make them into a class book.

Further work

Ask the children to fold a piece of paper in half and to draw on one half a picture of their own face when they were pleasing their friend and on the other half to draw a picture of their friend's face. Are they both smiling?

Share the pictures in Circle Time and talk about how they and their friend are feeling. Jot down these 'feelings' words and ask the children to add relevant ones to their picture – e.g. happy, willing, cheerful, merry, good. You could display these as pairs, or cut and mount them separately.

4. New friends, old friends

Ask the children to think about other friends – not necessarily children friends but new people who have just come into their lives. Ask them to close their eyes, to think of a new friend then to think of an old friend.

Stand and tell/Pass the sentence

Ask the children to stand up if they want to tell you about a new friend. Ask them to tell you something about this new friend. (Allow children to 'pass'.)

'My new friend is ... and ...'

Ask the children to stand up if they want to tell you about an old friend. Ask them to tell you something about this old friend. (Allow children to 'pass'.)

Auntie May is an old friend.
She saw me when I was a baby.

'My old friend is ... and ...'

Now ask them to think about friends who are older than they are – perhaps friends of their family, grandparents or new neighbours.

'A grown-up friend of mine is ... and ...'

Haiku

Read this haiku to the children and talk about what it means. Ask them to tell you words to write down about old and new friends. Help them to compose a haiku using some of these words. Ask them to vote with their feet to choose the one they like best.

New friends, old friends
I won't forget you
When a new friend comes to stay.
All friends are special.

Duplicate this haiku, give each child a copy and ask them to decorate it by drawing a picture or border around it. Choose a few to display.

Further work

Ask the children to draw their old and new friends and help them to add labels or captions to their pictures. This could make a two-part display – 'New friends, old friends'.

4. New friends, old friends

Ask the children to think about new friends – young or old people they have just met and who they know are going to be friends.

Pass the sentence

Ask each child to tell one thing about one of these new friends.

> 'My new friend is ... and I know we are going to be friends because ...'

This is my new friend Zoe.

I know we are going to be good friends because we like to play the same games and she lives near me.

Stand and tell

Now ask the children to think of some friend they have known for a long time – perhaps a friend of their parents. Ask the children if they can think of someone like this and would like to tell the group about this friend. Ask these children to stand and tell.

Pass the sentence

Now ask them to think of friends they had for a short time – 'little while friends'. perhaps they moved to a new house, or met them on holiday and may never see them again, but they will always remember them.

> 'I remember ... because ...'

Haiku

Use the haiku on the facing page and talk about it. Ask the children to suggest words to make two lists about new friends and old friends. Write these lists on the board. Ask the children to choose some of these or other words to compose and write down their own haiku. Share these in Circle Time.

Further work

Find books in the class or school library about friends such as *Orlando's Little-While Friends* by Audrey Wood (Child's Play, 1995) *or Wilfred Gordon McDonald Partridge* by M. Fox (Puffin Books, 1987).

Ask the children to draw and write about:

*   one character in the story
*   some friend they met once
*   an imaginary friend they would like to have had.

5. Quarrels

Talk about why people sometimes quarrel. Read this scenario:

> Meera and Tariq were really good friends and played well together but one day at school they both wanted to use the same crayon at the same time and they grabbed for it. They couldn't agree who should have it first; Meera pushed Tariq who started to cry. The teacher was not pleased.

Pass the sentence/Change places

Ask the children to think about how Meera and Tariq felt and ask each child to tell you how they think one of these children felt.

'I think Meera felt ...'
or 'I think Tariq felt ...'

Ask the children who repeat a word that has already been said to change places with the first person who said the word. (There will be many words repeated.)

I think Tariq felt:	I think Meera felt:
hurt	sorry
sad	unhappy
angry	cross
fed up	worried
cross.	bad.

Jot down

Jot down on paper any useful or appropriate words the children offer. When all the children have had a turn read out the words they told you. Write them large on a flip chart or chalk board under the headings 'Meera' and 'Tariq'. Read the words with the children – are any words in both lists?

Pass the face

Read the words again; ask the children to show by their face how Meera felt.
Pass the face around the circle.

Haiku

Read this haiku to the children. Use the two lists of words and help the children to compose a haiku.

Quarrels
Quarrels are horrid,
Such a waste of time and space.
Let's be friends instead.

Further work

Explore Meera's and Tariq's feelings and body language in drama sessions.

Ask the children to draw pictures about the story. Make a display of these together with haiku.

5. Quarrels

Explore the story of Meera and Tariq on the facing page. Ask the children to close their eyes and think about a time when someone they knew quarrelled. Ask them to think about how they themselves felt when someone quarrelled.

Pass the sentence/Change places

'When I saw someone quarrel I felt …' (Make sure they don't use people's names.)

Ask the children who repeat a word to change places with the last person who said it.

Pass the sentence/Jot down

Ask the children to think of their own quarrels and choose one of the following sentences to pass around the circle:

'When someone quarrelled with me I felt …'
'When I quarrelled with someone I felt …'

I'm quarrelling with you because I don't like what you did. It doesn't mean I don't like you.

Jot down these 'feelings' words on the board.

Explore these words by talking about:

- what they mean
- where else you can use them
- those that mean the same
- those that mean the opposite.

Explain that we all have these feelings from time to time but we must try to keep these feelings about what the child did and not about the child who did it.

Haiku

Talk with the children about the haiku on the facing page. Ask them to write their own haiku about quarrels; they can use words from the list of 'feelings' words to help them. Ask them to illustrate or decorate their haiku and make a display.

Further work

Ask the children to draw a picture of two friends having a quarrel and to write what the quarrel was about. Ask them to write two endings – a good ending where it all ended happily and another where it didn't end happily. Share the stories in Circle Time and make a list of all the ways that quarrels can end happily.

6. Making up

Remind the children about the story of Meera and Tariq and the words they told about the feelings of people who quarrel and ask them to think about what Meera and Tariq could do to be friends again.

Pass the sentence

Choose either of the following two sentences to pass around the circle

'Tariq could ...'
'Meera could ...'

There will be a lot of repetition here, but in essence someone has to say they are sorry.

Ask the children to think about different ways to say that they are sorry. Ask them to pass a 'sorry' sentence around the circle, using their own words and tones of voice.

Next ask the children to think of other ways that people can show they are sorry.

'You could ...'

> You could show you are sorry by:
>
> smiling at the person
> playing with them
> saying you won't do it again
> saying you didn't mean it
> asking how they feel
> asking them to play with you
> touching them gently
> being with them
> sharing your things
> thinking of them first.

Haiku

Read this haiku to the children. Ask for suggestions of other words that they could use in a 'making up' haiku and write these for the children to see. Help younger children to compose some haiku, using some of their words. Ask more mature children to work in groups to see if they can make their own group haiku. Write these up and help the children to learn some of them.

> **Making up**
> It's sad to break up.
> It's better when you make up.
> Let's be friends again.

Further work

Make a list of the ways children told you how we can show we are sorry and ask the children to choose one of the ways to illustrate and write about.

This could make a useful display which could be used when you need to help children to say they are sorry.

6. Making up

Remind children about the story of Meera and Tariq. Tell the children just saying 'sorry' is not enough; they have to show that they mean it.

Pass the sentence

Ask them to put themselves in Meera's place and to think what Meera could do to show she is sorry.

'If I were Meera, I would ...'

Ask the children to think about what Tariq could do to make it easy for Meera to say sorry.

Share ideas

Ask the children to work in small groups of four or five and think of a time when someone said they were sorry – in a story or on TV perhaps? Give two or three minutes for discussion before re-forming the group or circle.

Ask one person from each small group to volunteer to tell the circle what they have been talking about.

Haiku

Read the haiku on the facing page to the children. Ask them for their comments. Is it a good one to learn? Will it help them to stay friends? Ask pairs of children to work together to compose a haiku about staying friends or making up if they have fallen out of friends. Share these in Circle Time and choose a few for the children to illustrate and display.

Further work

Engage the children in a discussion about blame and fault and how difficult it is to make up sometimes. Talk about the need to make it easy for someone to say 'sorry'.

Ask the children to draw and write about Meera and Tariq making friends again or about how they made up after they had quarrelled with a friend. Tell them to use speech bubbles to show the words that the children actually said when making up the quarrel.

7. Making others happy

Tell the children that today they are going to be thinking about making other people happy. Ask them to think for a minute about how they make their families, friends, teachers, pets, or others happy.

Pass the sentence

'I make ... happy when I ...'

I make my kitten happy when I stroke her gently.

Change places

'Stand up all the people who can think of someone they made happy at home today.' Ask these children to change places with another.

Vary this by asking children to think of someone they made happy:

- at home
- in school
- in the class
- on the way to school
- in the playground.

Pass the sentence

'I made ... happy when I ...'

Haiku

Read this haiku to the children. Ask them to tell you words they could use in a haiku about making someone happy and write these words for the children to see. Help younger children to compose one or more class haiku; older children can work in groups to compose a group haiku.

> **Making others happy**
> What makes you happy?
> I'll find out how to do it.
> We'll always be friends.

Further work

Help children to make a list of words that describe being happy and to draw people or pets they can make happy.

In PE or drama, work on the theme 'How can you tell that people are happy?' Show how these people look, feel, move.

7. Making others happy

Ask the children to think about how they can make their friends happy.

Pass the sentence

Ask the children to tell one thing they do to make someone happy.

'I can … to make … happy.'

Write what the children say to use next in the 'change places' game.

Tidied up for Mrs Jones

Laid the table for Mum

Helped with my little sister

This is me

Let Sam go first

Shared crayons with Jim

Picked up the bricks

Waited my turn

Read a story with Rosie

Change places

When all the children have had the opportunity to tell, use the words from your list and ask the children to stand up and change places depending on what they said. Ask them to change places if they said, for example:

'I played with a friend'   'I listened to a grown-up'
'I talked with a friend'   'I comforted someone'.

Hands-up session – other people

Ask the children to think of the different kinds of people that they can make happy – such as people younger than themselves, people older, people who live near, people who live far away, people they like a lot and people they don't much like. Get them to raise their hand if they have suggestions to offer.

Make columns on the board and put labels on for these categories of people. Ask the children to tell you the kinds of things they could do to make these various people happy.

Haiku

Read the haiku on the facing page and talk about the words used. Ask the children to give you more words that would be good to use in a haiku about making people happy and write these up for all to see.

Ask them to work individually to compose a haiku about making people happy; share these in Circle Time. Select four or five of them and ask the children to vote with their feet to choose the one they think says it best. Write these neatly or on the computer to display.

Further work

Ask the children to draw a picture of themselves inside a circle and to write around their picture names of people they made happy this week. Able children could write more about what they did to make these people happy.

8. When friends move – separation

Sometimes good friends move away and new ones come. Ask the children to think of how they felt when someone they loved moved away. (If you can, relate this to a child or grown-up in the class or school who left.)

Pass the sentence/Jot down/Change places

'When ... left I felt ...'

Jot down the words they use – there will be many repetitions.

Ask the children who repeat words to change places with the last person who said the word.

Pass the face

Go around the circle asking the children to show the person next to them how these feelings look. (If children find this difficult, say, for example, 'How do you look when you are sad/miserable/angry/worried/missing them?')

Stand and tell

When all have had their turn, ask them to stand up if they can think of how the person moving away felt. Can they give you words for this?

You could collect and display these words.

Haiku

Read this haiku to the children. Ask them to tell you words they could use in a haiku about someone leaving them and moving away. Write these words for the children to see. Help younger children to compose one or more class haiku; older children can work in groups to compose a group haiku.

> **When friends move**
> Moving on is hard,
> Don't leave me, don't go away.
> I won't forget you.

Further work

Talk to the children about keeping in touch with old friends. Ask them how they can do this. Ask them to draw themselves keeping in touch with someone who moved away and about how they felt when they met them again.

Read *A New Home for Tiger* by Joan Stimson (Scholastic, 1997). It is in most school libraries.

8. When friends move – separation

(Sensitivity warning – You will know your children and when to do this activity. Be sensitive to the feelings of anyone who has suffered a bereavement. There is more on this in Theme 8: Loss, grief and separation.)

Pass the face

In some families, a parent, older sibling, grandparent or pet may have moved away and left the family home. Ask the children to show by their face how they feel when someone moves away.

Ask the children to tell you different ways to remember people who move away.

Pass the sentence

'The person left behind will feel ...'
'When someone goes away you can remember them by ...'

Ask the children to write a story about a child who moves to a new school and about how the children left behind feel about missing them. Ask them to include in their stories how the children left behind feel and ways in which they can keep in touch.

Haiku

Read the haiku on the facing page and talk about the words used. Ask the children to give you 'feelings' words that would be good to use in a haiku, about how people feel when they move away, or are left behind. List these feelings words. Ask the children to work together in pairs to compose two haiku – one on each theme. Share these in Circle Time, selecting some pairs to display.

The person left behind will feel...

• unhappy
• sad
• lonely
• fed up
• miserable

Further work

This could include making a list of things you could do to help you to keep in touch with someone who has gone away or ways to remember a friend who has moved away.

Ask them to read *Don't Forget to Write* by Martina Selway (Red Fox, 1993). It is in most school libraries.

Friends and Friendships
Let's celebrate friendship!

In Circle Time talk with the children about all the work they have done about friends and friendship. Praise them for their work and for their learning.

Pass the sentence

Ask the children to tell you what they have learned about being a good friend.

'I am a good friend when I ...'

Extension activities

Ask the children to draw a picture of themselves playing with one or more friends showing what they are doing to be a good friend. Help younger children to write a sentence about their picture and ask older children to write about it. Make a display of the children's pictures and writing.

Help them to write a class song or poem about being a friend and valuing friends and add these to the display. You might like to teach them the song 'Friends and Neighbours' (Malcolm Lockyer and Marvin Scott) recorded by Billy Cotton and his Band. The words can be found on the website http://lyricsplayground.com/alpha/songs/f/friendsandneighbours.shtml

Friends
Play together
Work together
Help each other out.

Friends are always there for you
Share for you
Care for you.

Never hurt or bother you
Never say bad things of you
Always looking out for you
Friends are all we need.

Collect all the storybooks you have about friends and friendship and add these to the display.

Use a drama session to ask the children to show how good friends look and behave. Ask older children to work in small groups to dramatise how someone is being a good friend and ask each group to present their drama to the whole circle.

Use this theme for an assembly; ask parents, visitors or another class to come and look at the children's work; present some of the dramas.

Theme 2 Growing and growing up

1. When I was very young

2. Now I am … I can …

3. Looking back

4. It takes time to grow

5. I know I'm getting bigger because . . .

6. Who helps us to grow and learn?

7. New responsibilities

8. Looking forward.

Explain to the children exactly what a haiku is. They don't have to abide by the 5-7-5 rule when they compose their own.

I am growing taller

A haiku is a:
Poem in three lines
Five syllables, then seven
Five again. No rhyme.

The following haiku can be used in this section:

When I was very young When I was little I couldn't do lots of things. Now I'm big, I can.	**I know I'm getting bigger because . . .** Bigger and better Every day in every way I am growing up.
Now I am … I can … I can draw pictures, I can read and write and spell. I learn every day.	**Who helps us to grow and learn?** Lots of people help. Mum and Dad and teacher too We can learn so much.
Looking back I remember things. Sad and happy memories Funny, good and bad.	**New responsibilities** New jobs we can do Now we're growing up so well, Helping everyone.
It takes time to grow Some things grow quickly But children take a long time. One day we'll be big.	**Looking forward** New work, new skills too. Growing up is fun for me, I can help myself.

1. When I was very young

Talk to the children about how they are growing and growing up all the time – you can't see that you're growing, but every day you grow a tiny bit more.

Pass the sentence

Ask the children to think of things they could do when they were very young.

'When I was very young I could ...'

Change places

Play the change places game:

- When a child repeats a word already given ask them to change places with whoever said it before.
- Wait until the end and ask those who said a certain word to stand up and then change places.

When I was younger I could...
cry
drink milk
crawl
sit up
sleep
go in a pram.

Pass the face

Ask the children to think of how they feel when the see a very young baby. Pass this face around the circle.

Touch your ...

Say to the children:

- touch your nose if you remember some of the nursery rhymes you learned when you were younger.
- touch your ears if you will sing one to the group.

Haiku

Read this haiku to the children. Ask them to help you to make a list of words they could use in a haiku about being very young or being a baby. Write these words for the children to see. Help younger children to compose one or more class haiku; older children can work in groups to compose a group haiku.

When I was very young
When I was little
I couldn't do lots of things.
Now I'm big, I can.

Further work

Ask the children to bring in photos of themselves as babies (and as they are now) and display these with labels and comments from the children.

Collect picture books from the library to read to the children and display – such as *The Trouble with Babies* by Angie and Chris Sage (Puffin Books, 1991) and *Aren't You Lucky!* by Catherine and Laurence Anholt (Red Fox, 1991).

1. When I was very young

Remind children that we all started out as tiny babies and ask them to think of what babies need to grow up healthy and happy.

Pass the sentence/Jot down

'I think a baby needs ...'

Jot down what they say – there will be some repetition. When everyone has had a turn read out what the children have told you.

Stand and tell

Ask the children if they can think of anything else.

If there are still some important things missing, talk about these (e.g. love, a loving home, grown-ups to take care of them, time to play).

I think a baby needs
milk to drink
someone to care for them
clothes
a pram
a bed
somewhere quiet to sleep
toys
someone to play with them
love
a loving home
people who care.

Vote with your feet

Look again at your list and ask the children to tell you which they think are the five most important things. Write these down on separate cards or paper. Place the cards around the room and ask the children to decide which they think is the most important. Ask them to go and stand by their choice. Make a list of these choices and the numbers of children who choose each.

Haiku

Read the haiku on the facing page and talk about the words used. Ask the children to give you more 'feelings' words that would be good to use in a haiku about being a baby. List these words. Ask the children to work in pairs to compose their own haiku, to write it out nearly and illustrate it. Ask each pair to read and show theirs in Circle Time.

Further work

Ask the children to vote on the three best haiku to display. Ask each child to write why they made this choice. Ask them to explain how the three were democratically chosen. Display some of this work with the three haiku.

2. Now I am (age) I can ...

Tell the children about some of the things you can do now that you couldn't do when you were their age. Ask them to think of something they couldn't do when they were very young, but can do now.

Pass the sentence/Jot down/Change places

'When I was very young I couldn't ... but I can now.'

Jot down each new thing they say to make a list.

Children who repeat words change places with the last child who said it. Read the list.

Stand, tell and sit down quickly

Ask the children to think of one thing they have just learned to do. Ask the children to do

When I was young I couldn't:
couldn't...
walk, stand, run, eat, drink from a cup, talk, sing, think

but I can now.

this quickly, telling everyone one thing that they can do now. If the children are quick at doing this, there will be a wave effect that ripples around the circle. (You may need to practise this.)

Stand and tell

Ask the children to think of how they learned to do these new things. Did someone teach them? Did they copy someone? Was it hard to learn? Ask them to think about one thing they learned and how they learned to do it. Ask volunteers to tell the group what they learned and how they learned to do it.

Haiku

Read this haiku to the children. Ask them to help you make a list of words they could use in a haiku about what they can do now they are growing older. Write these words for the children to see. Help younger

Now I am ... I can ...
I can draw pictures,
I can read and write and spell.
I learn every day.

children to compose one or more class haiku; older children can work in groups to compose a group haiku.

Further work

Ask the children if they know any stories or poems about children growing up. Make a collection, read and display such books from the library. Include, if you have them, *Henry's Baby* by Mary Hoffman (Dorling Kindersly, 1993) and *Hasn't He Grown?* by John Talbot (Andersen Press, 1989).

2. Now I am (age) I can ...

Ask the children to close their eyes and think of one thing they can do now that they couldn't do one year ago.

Pass the sentence/Change places/ Jot down

Now we are in this class we can:

help younger children
show visitors around school
do better drawings
read harder books
make interesting things with junk.

We all like it better now we are this age.

'Now I am six (or seven) I can ...'

Children who repeat a word change places with the last person who said it.

Jot down what the children say. Read your list.

Stand and tell – how did they learn it?

Ask the children to think about how they learned to do these new things. Is it a new skill? Did someone teach them or did they find out for themselves? Did they have to practise until they could do it well? Ask volunteers to stand up and tell you how they learned this new skill.

Stand, tell and sit down quickly

Ask the children to think of one skill they would like to learn when they are older. They should stand up, try to say it with only one word then sit down again quickly.

Hands-up session

Ask the children to raise a hand if they like being the age they are now, rather than being younger. Count how many hands are up and ask them to work out how many would rather be younger.

Haiku

Read the haiku on the facing page and talk about the words used. Ask the children to help you make a list of all the things they can now do and ask each child to compose, write and illustrate their own haiku using these ideas. Ask volunteers to read and show theirs in Circle Time.

Further work

This could include making a display of what the children said.

Alternatively, ask the children to fold a piece of paper in half and head the two sides 'What I could do when I was five' and 'What I can do now I am six [seven]' and draw pictures with labels or writing.

3. Looking back

Ask the children to think of some of the things they told you they used to do when they were young; some of these things will be happy but some might be sad.

Pass the sentence

Ask them all to think of one really happy thing they can remember that happened when they were younger.

'I remember being very happy when ...'

Ask these children to think of a word to tell how they felt before they sit down. Make a list of these words.

I remember being very happy when my sister was born.

Pass the face

When all the children have had their turn, tell the children to show by their face how they felt. Pass the face with that expression round the circle.

Stand and tell

Now ask the children to think of some sad thing that they remember happening when they were very young and to stand up if they can remember something sad from long ago.

Ask these children to think of one word to tell how they felt and make a second list.

Haiku

Read this haiku to the children. With the children read the two lists of words and ask them to help you to choose words to use in a 'looking back' haiku. Draw a ring around these words. Help younger children to compose one or more class haiku; older children can compose their own haiku.

> **Looking back**
> I remember things.
> Sad and happy memories
> Funny, good and bad.

Further work

Ask the children to draw pictures and write out their haiku to take home. Children can choose to draw pictures about a very happy or sad memory. You could display these under the heading 'Memories'.

3. Looking back

Remind children of the Circle Time when they thought of things they could do when they were younger.

Touch your ...

Ask the children to think of their memories and to:

- touch their nose if they can think of a really sad memory
- touch their head if they can think of a really worrying memory
- touch their toes if they can think of a frightening memory
- touch their chin if they can think of a very funny memory.

Ask volunteers to tell you some of their memories.

Pass the sentence

Now ask them to think of a really special time when they were younger. It may have been a holiday, a birthday, Christmas or another special day, perhaps when they or someone they know achieved something.

'My really special day was ...'

My really special memory is when my brother learned to drive the car.

He took us all out for a drive without L plates.

Pass the face

Ask the children to find a partner. In pairs, one child thinks of any memory and makes a face to show how he felt. The other child then has to guess this feeling and copy the facial expression before his partner reveals what he was thinking about.

Stand and tell

Back in the group or circle ask those children who guessed what feelings the face showed to stand up and tell.

Haiku

Read the haiku on the facing page and talk about it. Ask the children to make a list of happy and sad words before asking them to compose, write and illustrate their own haiku, using some of these words or their own. Ask volunteers to read and show theirs in Circle Time.

Further work

Help children to make a memory book with a page for each age, illustrating the highs and lows. A class project could include work on various memories.

4. It takes time to grow

Explain that some animals or creatures grow up very quickly, but that children take quite a long time. Draw on your experience of the animal world (or on previous work with the children) and talk about how quickly, for example, a bird or puppy grows up to be independent of its parents.

Pass the sentence

Ask the children to think of the things that other creatures have to learn to do before they are grown up.

'... have to learn to ...'

Jot down

Write down what the children say and use this to make lists of what various animals have to learn before they are grown up.

Touch your ...

Ask the children if they know how old they have to be before they can do certain things.

- 'Touch your ears if you know how old you must be to go swimming on your own.'
- 'Touch your chin if you know how old you must be before you can go to work.'
- 'Touch your elbows if you know how old you must be before you can marry.'

Birds have to learn to:

eat
fly
find food
make nests.

Kittens have to learn to:

open their eyes
drink milk
eat
purr
run
find food
wash themselves.

Kittens grow into cats quickly.

Haiku

Read this haiku to the children. Ask them to help you to choose words to use in a 'takes time to grow' haiku. Help younger children to compose one or more class haiku; ask older children to work in groups to compose, write out and illustrate a group haiku.

> **It takes time to grow**
> Some things grow quickly
> But children take a long time.
> One day we'll be big.

Further work

Ask the children to collect and cut out from magazines pictures of animal families with their young, pictures of people at various ages. These can be mounted with the message that baby animals grow quickly into adult animals but that human babies take a long time to grow into adults.

4. It takes time to grow

Ask the children to think of how animals, birds and other creatures grow and what they have to learn to do before they leave their parents and look after themselves.

Go round the group or circle asking each child to tell what various animals have to learn to do before they are old enough to leave their mothers – e.g. 'Kittens have to learn to lap milk'.

Stand, count and sit down quickly

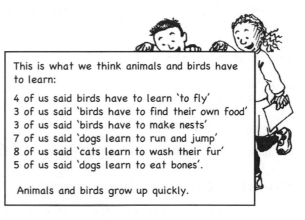

Play this game. All children stand. Ask those who said 'They have to learn to eat' to raise a hand; ask them to count themselves, you write down the number and only these children sit down.

Choose different sentences until all the children are sitting. This data would make a good display; add children's pictures or pictures from magazines.

> This is what we think animals and birds have to learn:
>
> 4 of us said birds have to learn 'to fly'
> 3 of us said 'birds have to find their own food'
> 3 of us said 'birds have to make nests'
> 7 of us said 'dogs learn to run and jump'
> 8 of us said 'cats learn to wash their fur'
> 5 of us said 'dogs learn to eat bones'.
>
> Animals and birds grow up quickly.

Hands-up session – what do humans do?

Ask the children to help you to make a list of all the things that human children have to do before they are ready to leave their mothers or carers to live on their own. They might say, for example, find or make a home, cook food, be trained in a job, find work. Get them to raise their hand if they have suggestions to offer.

Haiku

Read and talk about the haiku on the facing page. Ask the children for suggestions of words to use in a class haiku about it taking time to grow. List these. Ask each child to compose, write and illustrate their own haiku using these ideas or their own. Ask volunteers to read or show theirs in Circle Time.

Further work

Ask the children to draw and write about all the things a human child has to learn to do for itself before it is grown up.

Link this work with sex education, making sure that the children know that:

- it takes a man and a woman to make and have a baby
- boys grow up into men who can help to make babies
- girls grow into women who can have their own babies
- there is a lot to learn before they can do that.

5. I know I'm getting bigger because ...

Remind the children that they were babies once and are not babies any more – what happened? Talk to the children about growing bigger.

Pass the sentence/Change places

'I know I am getting bigger because ...'

Children who repeat a response can change places with the last person who said it.

Pass the sentence/Jot down

Ask them to tell you something that they can do now that they are bigger and are in school.

I know I'm getting bigger because:

My clothes are
too small.
I need new shoes.
I can do
more things.

'Now I am at school I can ...'

Jot down appropriate or interesting responses. Talk about these.

Stand, tell and sit down quickly

Ask the children 'Is being older better than being younger?' Tell them to stand, say 'yes' or 'no' and sit down quickly. This creates a wave effect.

Haiku

Read this haiku to the children and ask them to repeat it. Ask them to help you to choose and list words to use in composing their own haiku. Help younger children to compose one or more class haiku; ask older children to work in groups to compose, write out and illustrate a group haiku.

> **I know I'm getting bigger**
> Bigger and better
> Every day in every way
> I am growing up.

Further work

Duplicate the words of the class haiku for the youngest children and ask them to copy the writing below your writing. Ask them to illustrate the haiku with their own pictures. Display some of these.

Ask older children to copy out their group haiku and to illustrate it with drawings of children growing up and getting bigger.

Remind the children that it takes a long time and there is a lot to learn before children are grown up.

5. I know I'm getting bigger because ...

Tell children that we know they are growing bigger because they need larger clothes and are changing physically with new teeth, longer bones, etc.

Qustion and answer

Ask them to think of other ways they know they are growing up.

- What can they do now that they couldn't do before?
- What are they now allowed to do?

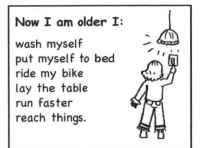

Now I am older I:

wash myself
put myself to bed
ride my bike
lay the table
run faster
reach things.

Pass the sentence

What are they allowed to do now they are growing up?

'Now I'm growing up I'm allowed to ...'

Change places

Play the change places game if children repeat what has been said.

Jot down

Write what the children say and when all have had a turn choose and read out six items from your list. Write them up somewhere for all to see.

Stand, count and sit down quickly

Now ask the children to think which is the most important of these six things they are now allowed to do.

I'm allowed
to stay up
late on
Saturdays.

Ask all children to stand. When you read out their choice, they go to the front, or the middle if you have a circle, and count themselves before going back to sit down. Write the number alongside each word to decide which the majority chose.

Haiku

Read and talk about the haiku on the facing page. Ask the children for their ideas of words to include in a haiku about getting bigger, growing up, learning new skills. List these. Ask the children to work in pairs to compose, write and illustrate one haiku using these ideas or their own. Ask volunteers to read and show theirs in Circle Time.

Further work

Ask the children to record, illustrate and display the data they generated in choosing the best six things they are now allowed to do.

6. Who helps us to grow and learn?

Ask the children to think about how they managed to learn all these new things that have helped them to grow and learn. Who helped them?

Pass the sentence

'... helps me to grow and learn'.

Jot down

There will be many repetitions but jot down what the children say, putting a tick for repeats. (All responses are correct – children may say words such as 'food' as well as people's names.) When all the children have had their turn, read out your list and tell the children how many of them gave that same answer.

Imagine it

Select the four most mentioned people from your list, write them up on the board and ask the children to close their eyes and think about what these people do to help them to grow and learn.

Stand and tell

Ask volunteers to choose one person to tell about.

Haiku

Read this haiku to the children and ask them to repeat it. Ask them to help you list words for a

> **Who helps us to grow and learn?**
> Lots of people help.
> Mum and Dad and teacher too
> We can learn so much.

class haiku about how they grow and learn. Help younger children to compose one or more class haiku; ask older children to work in groups to compose, write out and illustrate a group haiku.

Further work

Ask the children to draw a picture of a person who has helped them to learn to do something and you can help them to write a label or caption about their drawing. Older children can write for themselves about something they learned to do and how they managed to do it.

> My sister helps me to read my book.

> Mum helps me to get dressed.

> Dad helps me to ride my bike.

6. Who helps us to grow and learn?

Stand and tell

Ask the children to think of how they learn new skills. Ask volunteers to stand and tell.

Ask them to think of all the people who are helping them to grow and learn new things.

The swimming instructor is helping me to learn to swim.

Like this

Question and answer

Start the game which can go round the circle.

'Who is helping you to grow and learn new things?'
'My sister is helping me. Who is helping you?'

There will be some repetition; they may need help – remind them of people at home as well as those involved in out of school activities such as swimming, football, sewing, cooking, gym, football, other clubs.

Stand and mime

Ask for volunteers to mime what someone is helping them to do. Children who think they can guess stand up. The child miming can select children to answer until someone says the correct answer.

Haiku

Read and talk about the haiku on the facing page. Ask the children for their ideas of words to include in a haiku about people who help them to learn new skills. List these. Ask the children to work individually to compose, write and illustrate one haiku using these words from the list or their own. Ask volunteers to read and show theirs in Circle Time.

Further work

Ask the children to list the job titles of people who help them to learn new skills – e.g. the crossing patrol, the librarian, a teacher, a sports instructor, someone who runs an after school club, someone who helps with craft.

Ask them to work in small groups, each choosing a different person from the list to write about. Ask them each to illustrate what their chosen person does. Mount these together to make a group display.

7. New responsibilities

Ask the children to think about things they now do at home or at school which show that they are growing up. Tell the children that they will enjoy doing some of these things but that there may be things they don't like doing. Jot down what the children say for use during 'Further work'.

Pass the sentence/Change places

'I am growing up. I like to ...'

Play the change places game when children repeat an answer.

Group activity

Choose some of the things they said and play a version of 'touch your ...', for example:

> We like doing these things now we are growing up:
>
> going to bed later
> choosing what we eat
> helping in the kitchen
> playing out with friends
> watching TV later
> choosing new clothes
> helping with the baby
> helping with shopping
> choosing things.

- 'If you like being more grown up, stand up.'
- 'If you like helping at home, curl up small.'
- 'If you like tidying up, clap once.'
- 'If you can dress yourself, touch your nose.'

Add other new responsibilities as appropriate with activities such as wave your hand, touch your knee, stand on one leg, hop once.

Haiku

Read this haiku to the children and ask them to learn it. Ask them to help you make a list of words for a class haiku about their new responsibilities. Help younger children to compose one or more class haiku; ask older children to work in pairs to compose, write out and illustrate a joint haiku.

> **New responsibilities**
> New jobs we can do
> Now we're growing up so well,
> Helping everyone.

Further work

Discuss what the children said in the first part of this activity. Ask them to group their original responses into 'What I like doing very much' and 'What I don't like doing'.

Ask the children to find pictures of children helping. They can tear or cut these out to make a collage picture – 'Children are growing and growing up'. Add your own questions in speech bubbles such as 'Who is helping to cook?' 'Can you do some of these things?' 'What can you do to help?'

7. New responsibilities

Before Circle Time ask the children to draw two pictures of themselves doing:

- one new thing that they like doing to help now they are growing up
- one new thing they have to do – but may not like doing very much.

Ask the children to bring their pictures to the group or circle to remind them what they are going to say.

Pass the sentence

'I like doing ... but I don't like doing ...'

Jot down

Note the things that the children do like doing so that you can talk about these when all the children have finished.

Stand, tell and sit down quickly

Ask the children 'Do you like having these new responsibilities?' Tell them to stand, say 'yes' or 'no' and sit down quickly. This creates a wave effect.

Talk to the children about new responsibilities they will have as they are growing up and how there will be more of these as they grow and move through school.

Things we can do to help now we are growing up:

tidying up
helping to lay the table
putting our clothes away
remembering messages
answering the phone
working in the garden
reading to my little brother.

Haiku

Read and talk about the haiku on the facing page. Ask the children to suggest words about new responsibilities or jobs and list these. Ask the children to work in pairs to compose, write and illustrate two haiku, using the words from the list or their own. One haiku is to be about a responsibility they like and the other about something they don't like having to do. Ask volunteers to read and show theirs in Circle Time.

Further work

Make a double display using the children's haiku – one half about responsibilities they like and the other about responsibilities they don't like. Ask them to suggest speech bubbles to add to the display.

8. Looking forward

Is there something that you are learning (and are looking forward to being able to do) that you could tell the children about? Ask the children to think of some of the things that children in the next class (or that they in a year's time)

> **We look forward to:**
>
> playing in the big playground – 8
> going to the big library – 7
> looking after the little ones – 3
> choosing what we have for dinner – 2
> joining cubs/brownies – 10.

can do. Ask them to think of one thing that they are looking forward to being able to do.

Stand and mime

Can any of them show what their chosen skill or activity is?

Children can do this at the front (or in the middle of the circle) – perhaps several at the same time. Ask those watching in the circle to guess what the children are doing.

Pass the sentence

'When I am [five, six or in the next class] I will be able to ...'

Vote with your feet

Chose four or five of these new skills or activities and write them up on separate cards. Ask the children to decide from your cards which is the thing they most look forward to being able to do.

Put the cards in different places in the classroom and tell children to show, by standing near the card, which of these things they most look forward to doing. Ask each group to count its members; note the number on the card.

Haiku

Read this haiku to the children and talk about new work and new skills. Ask them to give you words about their new responsibilities that they can use in a class haiku. Help younger children to compose one or more class haiku; ask older children to work individually to compose, write out and illustrate a haiku.

> **Looking forward**
> New work, new skills too.
> Growing up is fun for me,
> I can help myself.

Further work

Pin up the cards to make a display of the children's choices. Ask them to write their names to display alongside their chosen activity. Add a title such as 'We want to learn to do these.'

Ask the children to think about and draw themselves doing something that they would like to do or be when they are fully grown up.

8. Looking forward

Ask the children to think of what skills they look forward to being able to master. Talk about physical skills – e.g. cycle riding, swimming, skipping; academic skills – e.g. reading, maths, writing; and co-operative skills – e.g. taking responsibility for yourself, others or possessions. Remind the children that growing up includes all three of these areas.

Draw three boxes on the board and label them 'skills', 'learning', 'responsibility'.

Pass the sentence

'I look forward to the time when I ...'

As each child finishes the sentence ask the group to decide which box it fits into. Either write the words or make a mark in the relevant box. Do some go in more than one box?

Stand, count and sit down quickly

When all the children have had their turn ask them to choose which of the three areas of growing up

I look forward to learning about the Greeks. This will be learning.

I look forward to the time when I can go out at night with my friends. This will be a responsibility.

I look forward to being able to swim. This will be a new skill.

they think is the most important. Play this game to collect data. Write down the number who chose each area and talk about why they made these choices.

Haiku

Read and talk about the haiku on the facing page. Ask the children to suggest 'feelings' words about 'looking forward' and list these. Ask them to work in pairs to compose, write and illustrate a haiku, using at least one 'feelings' word, either from the list or their own.

Further work

Ask each child to make a 'I am growing up' book, with pictures of themselves doing the activities they most look forward to being able to do.

Make a display using three overlapping circles with three headings: 'skills', 'learning', 'responsibilities'. Put pictures and quotes from children in the appropriate circle. If some fit into more than one circle, use the space where the circles overlap.

Read *Leaving Mrs Ellis* by Catherine Robinson (Red Fox, 1997). It is in most school libraries.

Let's celebrate growing and growing up!

In Circle Time talk with the children about all the work they have done about growing and growing up. Admire the illustrations and the writing. Praise them for their work and for their learning.

Pass the sentence

Ask the children to tell you what they have learned about growing and growing up.

'I know I am growing up when I ...'

Extension activities

Ask the children to draw a picture of themselves doing something that shows they are responsible for something at home. Help younger children to write a sentence about their picture and ask older children to compose their own writing about it.

Make a display of the children's pictures and writing.

Help them to write a class poem about growing and growing up and add these to the display. Can they choose a song tune they know well and write new words about growing up to fit the music?

If you're growing and you know it, clap your hands

Use a drama session to ask the children to mime themselves doing some of their new responsibilities and jobs. Encourage the children to work in groups to show their mimes to the rest of the class. Can the other children guess what they are doing?

Use this theme for an assembly; ask parents, visitors or another class to come and look at the children's work; present some of the mimes.

Theme 3 Keeping safe

1. Who am I?
2. Who keeps me safe?
3. I can keep myself safe
4. At home
5. Outside
6. Keeping my body healthy and safe
7. People I need to keep safe from
8. Our messages about keeping safe.

I can keep myself safe.

Explain to the children exactly what a haiku is. They don't have to abide by the 5-7-5 rule when they compose their own.

> **A haiku is a:**
> Poem in three lines
> Five syllables, then seven
> Five again. No rhyme.

The following haiku can be used in this section:

Who am I?	**Outside**
I know I am me,	There are safe places,
Not the same as you or her.	Where we can run, jump and play.
We are all unique.	Keep away from harm.
Who keeps me safe?	**Keeping my body healthy and safe**
Mum, dad, family,	Eat, drink, exercise!
People in the neighbourhood,	I must keep me safe and well.
They all keep me safe.	My body is mine.
I can keep myself safe	**People I need to keep safe from**
Lots of people help,	Some people can hurt.
But it's really down to me.	Say no, shout, kick, run away.
I keep myself safe.	Play with friends you know.
At home	**Our messages about keeping safe**
Things aren't dangerous.	Keep safe, keeping safe,
It's how we use them that counts.	Use your head and don't do wrong.
We have to take care.	You keep yourself safe.

Keeping safe - younger children

1. Who am I?

Tell the children that it is important to remember who they are, where they live and their phone number.

Question and answer

Ask the children to pass this question and answer round the circle. Start by saying your name to the first child:

'My name is ...Who are you?'

Stand up if ...

Ask the children to stand up if they can remember their address. Ask these children to say their address. If correct, they should stand inside the circle and then count themselves. (Start with one child saying 'one', the next 'two' and so on.)

Touch your ...

- 'Touch your ears if you remember your telephone number.' (Count how many.)
- 'Touch your nose if you can remember your birthday.'
- 'Put your elbows together if you can remember the name of our school.'
- 'Put your hands round your back if you can think of another safe house as well as where you live.'

Haiku

Read this haiku to the children. Talk about how they are all unique and special. Ask them to help you to make a class haiku. Duplicate these and ask the children to illustrate and decorate them. Ask older children to compose, write out and illustrate their own 'Who am I?' haiku. Display some of these.

> **Who am I?**
> I know I am me,
> Not the same as you or her.
> We are all unique.

Further work

Ask the children to close their eyes and think about their house and what it looks like. Ask them to draw a picture of themselves outside their house. Help them to write their name and something about themselves.

Ask them to draw themselves at their last birthday party, to draw the cake with candles and write their birth date.

1. Who am I?

Stand and show

Before Circle Time ask the children to write their full name and draw their home with the correct colour of front door. Ask them to draw themselves and all the people who live in their home. Can they put the number or name on the door and write their address and phone number? In Circle Time ask two or three children at a time to stand up and show their picture.

Then ask all children to:

Do you?

- kneel on one knee if they can say all their names
- stand up if they can say all their address
- wave one hand if they can say their phone number
- jump three times if they can tell you another safe place as well as their own home.

We know all these safe places:

Grandma's house
The lady next door's house
School
Church
Police station
Our shop.

Pass the sentence

(Remind children that they can say 'I don't know'.)

'Another safe place is ...'

Haiku

Read and talk about the haiku on the facing page. Remind them it's about who they are – someone special and unique. Ask them, in their groups, to work individually to compose one haiku each. Ask them to write theirs neatly and to mount and illustrate it before displaying all the groups' haiku together on one large piece of paper. Display these.

Further work

It could be necessary for a child to describe their adult or a lost sibling. Ask them to draw a friend and write a description of them. They could describe (orally or in writing) a child who is out of sight, a teacher or other well-known adult at school, a parent or member of their family.

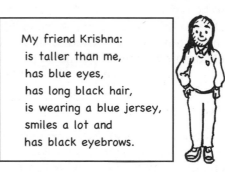

My friend Krishna:
is taller than me,
has blue eyes,
has long black hair,
is wearing a blue jersey,
smiles a lot and
has black eyebrows.

Play a describing game. Ask one child to volunteer to be described and to stand in the centre of the circle. Collect adjectives from volunteers in the circle to build up a description of the child in the centre.

2. Who keeps me safe?

Ask the children to think of people who keep them safe.

Pass the sentence/Change places

You can start by turning to the nearest child and saying:

> '... keeps me safe. Who keeps you safe?'

Children who repeat a response change places with the child who said it last. Many children will name family members, so only note down categories of people to make a list.

People who keep us safe

Our families
The police
The crossing patrol
Our teachers
Doctors
Nurses
Bus driver.

Stand and mime

Name a person (e.g. police officer) from your list and ask the children to think of what this person does to keep us safe. Ask them to stand up in turn and show (mime) what the person does. (Change the person as you go round the circle so that you get through the list.)

Pass the sentence

> 'My sister [or friend, police officer, crossing patroller, etc.] keeps me safe when ...'

Haiku

Read this haiku to the children. Talk about and read the list again of all the people who keep them safe. Choose one person from the list and ask the children to help you to make a class haiku about that person. Do several of these and ask the children to copy out the writing and to decorate their work. Ask older children to compose, write out and illustrate their own 'Who keeps me safe?' haiku to display.

Who keeps me safe?
Mum, dad, family,
People in the neighbourhood,
They all keep me safe.

Further work

Ask the children to draw one person from your list who keeps us safe. Help them to write a label or sentence for their picture about how these people keep us safe. Older children may be able to write a good description of the person and how doing their job well helps to keep people safe.

2. Who keeps me safe?

Before Circle Time ask the children to think of people who keep them safe and to work in groups of three or four to make a combined list. In Circle Time ask one of each group to name the people they wrote down. Choose a scribe who can write these people's names (or jobs) on the board as each group reads their list.

When all the children have had their turn, look down the list and ask each group to choose one person and think how they can show (act out) this person at work. Send the small groups of children to different parts of the classroom to practise how they will do this – allow no more than four minutes.

Stand and mime

In turn ask each group to act out their chosen person showing what they do to keep people safe. Ask the children from the circle to touch their nose when they think they have guessed the job. Allow no more than two guesses before asking the actors to tell.

Haiku

Read and talk about the haiku on the facing page. Remind them it's about people whose job it is to keep them safe. Ask them, in their groups, to work individually to compose a haiku about a different person. Ask them to write theirs neatly and to draw the person doing their job. Ask each group to make the pictures and haiku into a strip display on one long piece of paper. Display these.

Further work

Arrange visits from people such as the school nurse, police and fire officers, road safety officers, etc.

Ask the children to work together to make a collage of people who help to keep us safe.

Ask the children to work in pairs to write about and illustrate one of these people.

These people help to keep us safe:

Our families   The police   Our teachers   Nurses   Crossing patrol   Childminder

3. I can keep myself safe

Tell the children that they have a job too – to help the people who keep them safe. Ask them to think of all the things they can do to help various people such as the crossing patroller, police officer, store official, warden, doctor, teacher.

Pass the sentence

Choose one of these sentences to pass:

> 'I can help by ...'
> 'I can help my teacher [grandma, etc.] to keep me safe by ...'

This is Shiulie keeping safe going shopping.

I am holding Mum's hand.

Jot down

Ask the children to think of places where they play and list these.

Now ask the children to think for you how they keep themselves safe in these locations. You may need to add other places to your list – e.g. their bedroom, garden, kitchen, classroom, playground, park, seaside, forest, street.

Pass the sentence

Choose different locations so that you get through the above list.

> 'I keep safe in my bedroom [my garden, etc.] by ...'

Haiku

Read this haiku to the children. Talk about and read the list again of all the places where they play and need to keep themselves safe. Choose one place from the list and ask them to help you to make a class haiku about keeping safe in that place. Do several of these and ask

> **I can keep myself safe**
> Lots of people help,
> But it's really down to me.
> I keep myself safe.

the children to copy out the writing and to decorate their work. Ask older children to compose, write out and illustrate their own 'I keep myself safe' haiku to display.

Further work

Ask the children to draw themselves keeping safe in one of these places. Are they helping someone to keep themselves safe or are they on their own? Ask them to tell you what they are doing. Write what they say on their picture or in a speech bubble on coloured paper alongside so that everyone can read it.

3. I can keep myself safe

Change places

Remind children that they have an important part to play in keeping themselves safe.

I remember walking along a high wall and I fell off.
This was doing something that didn't keep me safe.

Ask the children to stand up and change places if they can:

- remember doing something that kept them safe
- remember doing something that didn't keep them safe
- remember doing something that hurt someone else.

Pass the sentence

Ask them to think of one thing they can do that will keep them safe.

'I can ... to keep myself safe.'

Tell a story

Azif was leaning out of a car window without a seat belt on as it drove down the High Street. Alice and Paco had a little dog and wanted to cross the road to go to the shop. Ben had his ball on the ground and was kicking it about as he walked to the park. Jo thought he would cross the road between some parked cars.

I would tell Azif to close the car window and put his seat belt on.

Share ideas

Divide the group or circle into four parts and ask each part what they would say to one of the named children. Give the children a few minutes to discuss this in their groups.

Stand and tell

Ask for volunteers to tell the circle what they would say.

'I would tell Azif ...', 'I would tell Ben ...', 'I would tell Jo ...', etc.

Haiku

Read and talk about the haiku on the facing page. Remind them that it's about keeping themselves safe. Ask them, in their groups, to work individually to compose a haiku about a different place where they need to keep safe. Ask them to write theirs neatly and to draw the place. Ask each group to make the illustrated haiku into a strip display on one long piece of paper to display.

Further work

Explore the above story through role play in drama sessions. Ask the children to rewrite the story, with the children all keeping themselves safe.

4. At home

Pass the sentence

Tell the children that their home is a safe place but they must still take care not to do anything that could hurt themselves or other people. Ask the children to think of where they play inside their homes.

'I play in ...'

We can play:

in the sitting room
in the hall
in the kitchen
in the bedroom
in the dining room
on the stairs.

Jot down

There will be many repetitions, but jot down each room the children mention. Make a list of these rooms on the board and ask the children to think about the safest places inside their homes to play.

Stand up if ...

Ask the children to stand up if they think the kitchen (use other places from your list) is the safest place. Jot down the numbers of children who stand up for each room.

When you have gone through all the rooms on your list, ask the children which room they now think is the very safest place to play in their house.

Touch your ...

Go through the list again this time asking children to touch their nose when you say the place they think is the least safe place to play in their homes. Will they say the stairs? Talk about how it can be unsafe to play on the stairs.

Haiku

Read this haiku to the children. Talk about their role in keeping safe at home and using things safely. Ask children to help you to compose one haiku about each room on the list.

At home
Things aren't dangerous.
It's how we use them that counts.
We have to take care.

Further work

Ask the children to draw themselves playing in a safe place in their home. Make a large picture of the inside of a house, showing all the rooms. Ask (or help) children to draw and cut out a picture of themselves to place in the safe rooms. Write 'safety' questions on large speech bubbles, such as 'Is it good to play here?'

4. At home

Imagine it

Ask the children to think of safe things in their own homes which could be dangerous if they were not used properly. Give an example, such as; a pair of scissors is a safe thing to use to cut something carefully, but not to stick into someone. Ask the children to work in pairs or fours and to make a quick list of things which are really safe if used carefully but could be harmful if not used correctly. Allow two minutes for this.

Stand and tell

Ask each group to tell everyone one thing from their list that has not already been said and to cross off things as they are mentioned. You could ask a scribe to write these up.

When all children have had their turn ask the children to stand and tell if they still have something on their list.

Stand and tell

Ask for volunteers to tell the group what they would say to someone who was using one of these objects in an unsafe way.

'I would say ...'

Keep yourself safe

Keep scissors closed in your hand.
Don't walk about with a knife.
Keep away from electric plugs.
Use things in the proper way.
Anything could be unsafe if not used properly.
Keep away from hot things.

Haiku

Read and talk about the haiku on the facing page. Remind them it's about using things safely. Ask them, in their groups, to work in pairs to compose two haiku about two objects that they must use safely. Ask them to write theirs neatly and to draw the object. Can they mount these for display?

Further work

Ask the children to write a list of advice about using things safely in their homes.

5. Outside

Pass the sentence/Change places

Tell the children that there are safe and unsafe places to play outside. Ask them to think of the safe places.

'A safe place to play is ...'

Change places for repeats.

Jot down

Ask volunteers to tell you where they go and make a list of the places they mention – e.g. seaside, park, riverside, theme park, zoo, picnics, barbecues – include local places.

Don't go too near the BBQ. It is hot.

Pass the sentence

'At a BBQ you keep safe by ...'

Change the location after three or four children have answered and list any appropriate responses.

Read through the list to remind the children of what they have told you and talk about each one.

Haiku

Read this haiku to the children. Talk about the safe places where they play outside their home. Choose one place from the list and ask them to help you make a class haiku about keeping safe there. Do several of these. Ask older children to compose, write out and illustrate their own 'Safe outside' haiku to display.

> **Outside**
> There are safe places,
> Where we can run, jump and play.
> Keep away from harm.

Further work

Remind the children of the list of places where they go and ask them to draw a picture of themselves with other people in one of these places. Help them to write a 'keeping safe' message on their picture. Make these into a book, using each piece of work as a page. Ask the children to suggest a title – such as 'Keeping safe outside'.

5. Outside

Pass the sentence

Remind the children that even in safe places there can be dangers.
Ask them to tell you what could be unsafe in their garden. Then choose other places – such as a road, playground, park, seaside.

'It could be unsafe in (or at) ... if you ...'

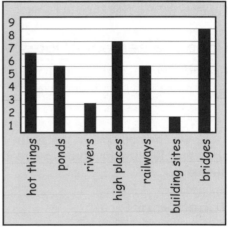

Jot down

List some of the dangers they tell you on separate sheets of card or paper. When all children have had their turn read out what you have written – e.g. hot things, ponds, rivers, high places, railways, building sites, bridges, etc.

Vote with your feet

Spread the cards around the classroom and tell children to stand near the card of their choice to show which of these things they think is the most dangerous. Ask each group to count its members and note down the total against the danger.

Now ask one child from each group to hold the card with the rest of their group behind them to make a 'living chart'.

Haiku

Read and talk about the haiku on the facing page. Remind them it's about places outdoors which are usually safe. Ask them to work in their groups and choose two places which are usually safe. Ask them to make a list of things which could become unsafe in both these places if people didn't take care. Ask each child in the group to compose and illustrate their own haiku about one place. Display the whole group's haiku together with their lists alongside.

Further work

Remind the children about the data they generated on the cards about the dangers. Ask them to make a 'pictorial representation' of that data by labelling columns on a chart and drawing their face to put in the column of their choice. Ask them to label the display and write what the data show. Ask them to draw and write about how they keep safe in one of these locations.

6. Keeping my body healthy and safe

Stand and tell/Jot down

Ask the children to stand and tell if they know what 'healthy' means. Jot down responses from these children and discuss them. Because 'healthy' is a difficult concept, you may need to help them to understand that 'healthy' means getting fit, keeping themselves safe and well.

Pass the sentence/Jot down

Ask the children to tell you what they can do to make and keep themselves healthy.

  'I can ...'

Jot down the appropriate things they say and when all have had their turn read out the list.

To keep your body healthy you can:

eat good food
run about
play games
sleep
drink water
keep yourself clean
wash your hair
clean your teeth twice a day.

Touch your ...

  'Touch your nose if you can think of any more to add to the list.'

Read the list and choose one of the things the children said and allow them to elaborate on it. For example, if they said 'You have to exercise', ask the children to tell you some of the ways they do this.

Haiku

Read this haiku to the children. Talk about their own role in keeping their body healthy and safe. Explain that we need to eat and drink well, exercise, rest and keep clean.

Choose 'exercise' and ask the children to help you to make a class haiku about it. Choose different aspects of health and compose other class haiku. Ask older children to compose, write out and illustrate their own haiku to display.

> **Keeping my body healthy and safe**
> Eat, drink, exercise!
> I must keep me safe and well.
> My body is mine.

Further work

Ask the children to draw themselves doing something that makes and keeps them healthy. Either use their drawings to make a large picture and mount them individually or send them home with the message that you are learning about how to keep healthy.

6. Keeping my body healthy and safe

Before Circle Time ask all the children to draw a healthy person. Ask them to write around the picture what their person can do to make themselves healthy and keep themselves healthy.

Stand and tell

Ask the children in turn to show their pictures and tell one of the things they wrote down. (Remember to allow children to 'pass' if they wish.)

Jot down

Make a list of the healthy activities the children have mentioned. Read the list to the children when all who wish to have had a turn. Perhaps these activities can be grouped together under categories such as food, exercise, drink, rest, cleanliness, medical help. Emotional well-being covers love or friendship.

Share ideas

Divide the children into groups, giving each group one of the above categories to explore. Allow the groups to have a few minutes to share ideas and then come together in the circle again.

Stand and tell

Ask each group in turn to tell the others what they think is important about their category. Invite children from the circle to add ideas.

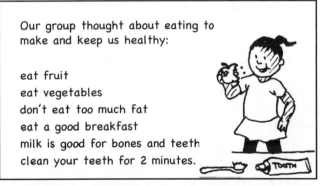

Our group thought about eating to make and keep us healthy:

eat fruit
eat vegetables
don't eat too much fat
eat a good breakfast
milk is good for bones and teeth
clean your teeth for 2 minutes.

Haiku

Read and talk about the haiku on the facing page. Remind them that it's about keeping their body healthy and safe. Ask them to work in their groups and write a haiku about each aspect of keeping healthy and safe. Ask them to illustrate these and display them.

Further work

Ask the children to think of any other things that affect our well-being. They may offer such things as having friends or pets, being loved, being part of a family, thinking of others and learning new skills. They may mention things you shouldn't do – such as smoking, drinking alcohol or taking drugs.

7. People I need to keep safe from

Remind the children of people who keep them safe (from 'Who keeps me safe?' earlier in this theme). Explain that they might need to keep themselves safe from some children or adults.

> I keep myself safe from children who:
>
> play football
>
>   push
>
> run fast
>
>   want to fight
>
> don't look where they're going
>
>   bully people.

Touch your ...

Ask the children to:

- touch their ears if they have ever been hurt by an adult
- touch their shoulders if they have ever been hurt by a child.

Pass the sentence

Explain that sometimes people don't mean to hurt – it sometimes happens by accident. Ask them to think about the school playground when there are lots of children playing games.

'In the playground I keep myself safe from [or by] ...'

Make a list of what they say; afterwards read and discuss their list.

Pass the sentence

Ask the children to think of people outside school whom they might need to keep safe from. Remind them about people who might want to take them away and hurt them; they must only go with people who they know are safe.

'I go home from school with ...'

Haiku

Read this haiku to the children. Talk about their role in keeping themselves safe. If they get into difficulties with someone they don't know, they must shout, kick and run away from them. Help children to make a class haiku about keeping safe from people, whether they know them well or not.

> **People I need to keep safe from**
> Some people can hurt.
> Say no, shout, kick, run away.
> Play with friends you know.

Further work

Extend this by talking about what they must do if someone they don't know wants to take them home or brings a message that might not be true. Talk about good and bad touches and remind them that their body is theirs and they are in charge of who touches them.

It may be appropriate here to discuss your school's policy about bullying.

7. People I need to keep safe from

Ask the children to think of people who might want to harm them or take them away; remind them that they must take charge if they think someone might want to do this. Make sure they know what to do if this happens to them – e.g. say no, shout loudly, run away, find a safe adult, find a safe place.

Things to say to a bully:

No
Go away
That's wrong
No, I'm not going to
I'm not afraid of you
I shall tell a grown-up.

Pass the sentence

'If a grown-up tries to hurt me or take me away, I must ...'

Pass the sentence

Ask the children to think of other children who might want to harm them or other children – bullies. Find out what they know about bullies and if they know what to do. Divide the class into two and use one of these 'pass the sentence' techniques with each half:

'A bully is someone who ...'

'If someone tries to bully me, I must ...'

Stand and tell

Ask the children to work in groups to think of a slogan that will tell everyone what to do if they are bullied. Ask someone from each group to tell the class. Write down their slogans and ask them to choose the one they think is most likely to succeed and to vote for the one they think is best. If no one is able to think of a slogan, try to work one out with them – e.g. 'If someone bullies you, tell and keep on telling until someone listens.'

Haiku

Read the haiku on the facing page. Remind them that it's about what to do if someone tries to harm them. Ask the children to work in pairs and write a haiku about keeping safe from people. Ask them to illustrate and display them.

Further work

Ask the children to fold a piece of paper into two. Ask them to draw two pictures – one of someone who is being bullied and to write what is happening, the other a picture of someone helping a person who is being bullied. Use a speech bubble for their words. Ask the children to take the work home to show their families, or use it to make a wall display.

8. Our messages about keeping safe

Pass the sentence/Change places

Remind the children about all the work they have done about keeping themselves safe – at home, in school, from dangerous places and dangerous people. Ask the children to think of a message to give to other children to keep them safe.

'I would say ...'

If they repeat what has been said, ask them to change places with the last person who said it.

> **'Keeping safe' messages**
>
> Look where you're going
>
> Don't bump into people
>
> Hot things burn
>
> Rivers can be deep
>
> Take care near water
>
> Be careful near strange dogs.

Jot down

Make a list of what the children say, then read out their messages.

Focus on a few, say three or four, of the most appropriate messages and ask the children to choose one message that they think says it best.

Vote with your feet

Read out each of the three or four messages and ask the children who think that one is the best for them to stand up and say 'I think this is the most important message for me.' Ask these children to count themselves. Make a display of the children's messages and read them with the children frequently.

Haiku

Read this haiku to the children. Talk about the different messages they would give to other children to help to keep themselves safe. Ask them to help you to make a class haiku with a message about keeping safe. Ask older children to compose, write out and illustrate their own haiku to display.

> **Our messages about keeping safe**
> Keep safe, keeping safe,
> Use your head and don't do wrong.
> You keep yourself safe.

Further work

Ask the children to think of some time they were hurt. Ask them to decide whether this was their own fault, perhaps because they were not keeping themselves safe. Ask the children to draw a picture about what happened next. Help them to write a sentence about it.

8. Our messages about keeping safe

Stand, tell and sit down quickly

Ask the children to think about words that they would include in a 'keeping safe' message for the younger children in your school. It can be to do with any aspect of keeping safe. Make a list of their words and then read the list to the children.

This is our 'keeping safe' message

Play in a safe place.

Pass the sentence/Change places/Jot down

Ask them to use some of these words in a good message.

'A good "keeping safe" message would be ...'

Write (or choose a scribe to write) the messages on the board. Number them.

Share ideas

Ask the children to leave the circle and go into their working groups. Ask each group to decide which, for them, is the best of the 'keeping safe' messages. Ask them to write down the number of the message together with any ideas of how they could make this into a display for younger children in the school. Allow only a few minutes for this activity.

Stand and tell

Come together as a whole class and ask a child from each group to tell everyone their message and how they could display it for younger children.

Haiku

Read the haiku on the facing page. Remind them that it's about taking responsibility for their own safety. Ask the children to work in pairs and write a haiku about the things they can do to keep themselves safe from all kinds of harm. Ask them to illustrate their haiku, display it on a table and then ask all the children to go around the tables reading each one. Ask them to vote with their feet for the one that they think is the best haiku.

Further work

Ask the groups to write out their messages and illustrate them.
Perhaps a small group of children could take their messages to show the younger children. They could then display them in an area of the school where everyone will see them.

Let's celebrate keeping safe!

In Circle Time talk with the children about all the work they have done about keeping themselves safe. Praise their illustrations and writing. Praise them for their work and for their learning.

Pass the sentence

Ask the children to tell you what they have learned about keeping themselves safe.

'I know that ...'

Ask the children to think about how to deal with children who might try to hurt them.

'I would ...'

Ask the children to think about how to deal with adults who might try to hurt them.

'I would ...'

Ask the children to think about how to deal with someone who might try to take them away.

'I would ...'

Extension activities

Help them to write a class poem or rap about keeping themselves safe. Can they learn it?

Use a drama session to ask the children to role play someone who is resisting an adult who is trying to take them away. What will they say? What will they do? (Don't ask them to role play the person trying to take them away.) Encourage the children to show their role plays to the rest of the class.

Use this theme for an assembly; ask parents, visitors or another class to come and look at the children's work and present some of the drama.

> **Our class rap**
>
> If someone tries to take me away,
> This is what I'd do,
> Shout and scream and make a fuss,
> Kick and hit and make a fuss,
> Make a, make a, make a fuss!
> This is what I'd do.
>
> So everyone will hear,
> So everyone will know,
> So everyone will hear and know
> And come to my res-cue!

Theme 4 **Self-esteem**

1. Names are important
2. Everyone is special
3. Body language
4. What I'm good at
5. Empathy
6. Working together.

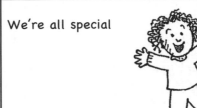

We're all special

Explain to the children exactly what a haiku is. They don't have to abide by the 5,7,5 rule when they compose their own.

A haiku is a:
Poem in three lines
Five syllables, then seven
Five again. No rhyme.

The following haiku can be used in this section.

Names are important Call me by my name. Don't call me silly names or It will make me mad!	**What I'm good at** When I don't feel good I think of things I'm good at. Then I feel better.
Everyone is special I feel good today. Everything is going well. I got a gold star.	**Empathy** Get inside their shoes! Can you get inside their skin? Think of how they feel.
Body language I know how you feel. Your body tells the story. Stand straight, breathe deep, smile.	**Working together** We help each other. Co-operation is good, Then we all do well.

1. Names are important

Talk to the children about names – first names and family names. Explain that years ago all ladies used to change their name when they got married to show that they belonged to a new family. Nowadays some ladies like to keep their old name. Talk about the choosing of a name for a baby and that this is often a time when the family has a special party or ceremony, sometimes a religious service.

My name is Brook.
I think my family
used to live
near a brook
or stream.

Stand and tell

Ask volunteers to talk about any christening or baptism or other religious service they have been to when introducing a new child into a religious family. Ask volunteers to tell about a party at home for a new baby.

Explain that our names are a part of us and a very important part. We must always use people's names properly and not shorten or change them unless the person asks you to do this. Some people like to have a nickname but some do not. It is polite to use peoples' names when talking to them. It makes them feel good when they know you have remembered their name.

Pass the sentence

'My name is ...'

Haiku

Read this haiku to the children. Remind them that using peoples' names makes them feel good. Help them to write one or more haiku about using peoples' names.

> **Names are important**
> Call me by my name.
> Don't call me silly names or
> It will make me mad!

Further work

Explain that years ago the first son in a family often had the same first name as his father – e.g. John's father would also be called John. Ask children to talk to their families about their first names. Are there any first names that many of the people in the family share? Are they themselves called after someone in their family? Can this cause a problem when they are together? Share what they find out in Circle Time.

1. Names are important

Explain to the children the importance of using peoples' names correctly. Talk about how people feel when people call them by the wrong name or get them mixed up with someone else. How does that make them feel?

Pass the sentence

'When people use my name I feel ...'

Stand and tell

Talk about nicknames and ask any children who have a nickname that their family uses to tell the class.

Ask these children if they would mind if everyone called them that name, or is it reserved for special people only?

Stand, tell and sit down quickly

Ask the children to think of nicknames that famous people have and if they can think of one, to stand. Ask them to say the nickname and sit down quickly. Do other children know these nicknames? Can any tell you how they came about?

> If people use my name I feel:
>
> great
>
> special
>
> they know me
>
> they've remembered
>
> I'm important
>
> I'm somebody
>
> they know who I am
>
> they like me
>
> I matter to them.

Remind the children that nicknames are personal and they must only use them if the people give their permission.

Haiku

Read the haiku on the facing page to the children. Remind them about the importance of using peoples' correct names. Ask each child to write and illustrate a haiku about the importance of peoples' names.

Further work

Explain that in the past family names were often used to tell about the work that the person did. Can the children tell you any? For example, a Smith used to work with iron, a Cooper used to work with barrels, a Forrester or Wood used to work in a forest or wood. Ask them to collect all the family names (surnames) that tell of the person's job. Ask them to get help from their families and share these names in Circle Time.

2. Everyone is special

Remind the children that we are all the same in
some ways and that we are all different in
others. Explain that we are all very special and
unique. Ask them to think of ways in which
they are different from other people in their
class because of the things they like to do, eat,
play, or because they have a special talent.

I am special
because
I can swim across
the pool.

Pass the sentence

'I am special because ...'

Jot down

Make a quick list of some of the things they say.

Pass the sentence/Change places/Jot down

Ask the children to think of some sport or physical activity they are really good at and
how they feel when they are doing this thing.

'I feel great when I ...'

Ask the children to change places if they repeat what someone else has said. Write
these things up on the board and afterwards read through the list.

Vote with your feet

Ask the children to choose just six of the things that the children said they were good at and
to decide which they most prefer doing from this list. Ask them to vote with their feet to find
out which is the most popular sport or activity. You could make a chart of the findings.

Haiku

Read this 'feeling good' haiku with the children and
ask them to help you compose one for your class.

Everyone is special
I feel good today.
Everything is going well.
I got a gold star.

Further work

Ask the children to draw a picture of their family and to say what is special about
everyone in their picture. Help them to write key words about this specialness.

2. Everyone is special

Remind the children that we are very special and unique. Explain that we are all good at some things and not so good at others and that we must remember the things we are good at while we are trying to get better at some of the things we are not so good at. Talk about being positive or negative about things. Tell them about some people seeing a glass as half empty and others as half full. Ask them to think of something positive about themselves that shows that they are special.

Something positive about me is that I can run very fast.

Pass the sentence/Change places

'Something positive about me is ...'

Ask those who repeat to change places with the last person who said it.

Jot down

Make a quick list of some of the things the children say. Talk about these things and later ask each child to make a list of all the positive things they can say about themselves.

Pass the sentence

Remind them that we have to try to get better at some things and ask them to think of one thing they are going to try to get better at doing.

'I am going to try to get better at ...'

Haiku

Read the haiku on the facing page to the children. Remind them that they are to think of positive things about themselves and the list they made. Ask each child to compose, write and illustrate a haiku about something positive about themselves.

Further work

Ask the children to talk to their families about the ways in which they are special. Ask them to write down what each person in their family says about them – e.g. 'Mum says I am special because I help her a lot and try to do as I'm told.'

3. Body language

Talk to the children about showing a confident appearance to other people.

I feel great when I score a goal in football.

Show how you feel

Ask them to think about how their body and face can show that they feel great today. Stand and pass this body and face language around the circle.

Repeat the above activity with a negative pose.

Pass the sentence/Jot down

Remind the children that their faces and bodies show their feelings and that they will feel better if they look positive. Talk about other ways of showing that they feel great and the kinds of things that make them feel great.

'I feel great when I ...'

Make a list of key words on the board and when all have had their turn talk about what they have said.

Hands-up session – praise

Talk to the children about praise and how it makes them feel when someone praises them for something they have done. Do they ever praise anyone? If they do, how does that make them feel when the person smiles? Ask them to raise their hand if they have suggestions to offer.

Haiku

Read this haiku to the children and ask them to help you compose a class one about positive body language. Use words from your list.

> **Body language**
> I know how you feel.
> Your body tells the story.
> Stand straight, breathe deep, smile.

Further work

In PE or movement sessions practise different kinds of body language – e.g. showing how they look when they are serious, hurt, happy, frightened, excited. Ask them to draw pictures of themselves showing different feelings.

3. Body Language

Talk to the children about the importance of presenting a confident appearance to other people. Explain that when people see how you look it helps them to know how you feel.

When I look positive I feel in charge of myself.

Pass the face

Ask them to think themselves into being really sad and to show by their face and body how they look. Pass this around the circle. Practise showing other feelings such as joy, excitement, love.

Pass the sentence/Jot down

Remind the children that they will always feel much better if their faces and bodies look positive. Explain that looking positive makes other people respect them and that they are less likely to be bullied if they present themselves as positive people.

  'When I look positive I feel ...'

Make a list of these key words on the board for later use in the haiku.

Imagine it

Ask each child to close their eyes and think how they feel when someone praises them. Talk about how the person doing the praising feels. Can volunteers give you some words to describe this?

Haiku

Read the haiku on the facing page to the children and ask them to help to compose a class one about body language. Use words from your list.

Further work

Ask the children to think about the last time they themselves praised one of their friends or family. Remind them that they can always find something good about someone to praise. Ask them to write about what happened. If they can't remember a time, ask them to write a story about someone who praised a grown-up, how this came about and what happened next. Display some of these under a heading such as 'Praise makes us look and feel good'.

4. What I'm good at

Tell the children about something that you are good at. Explain what you had to do to get good at this thing and about people or other things that helped.

I am good
at riding my bike.
I feel happy
when I ride it.

Pass the sentence

Ask the children to think of one thing that they are good at and how they feel when they are doing it.

'I am good at ... and when I'm doing it I feel ...'

Pass the face

Ask children to pass the face showing how they feel about this thing they are good at.

Stand and tell

Ask volunteers to say how they learned to do this thing and who and what helped.

Pass the sentence

Talk about how children learned to do this thing. Did someone help? Did they have a book about it? Did they go somewhere to learn it? Did they have to practise a lot?

'I learned to do ... by ...'

Haiku

Read this haiku to the children. Ask them to help you compose one about things they are good at. Can they compose several to make a wall display?

> **What I'm good at**
> When I don't feel good
> I think of things I'm good at.
> Then I feel better.

Further work

In movement sessions ask children to mime doing some of the activities they said they are good at. For example, call out 'riding a bike', 'making cakes', 'drawing a picture' and ask the children to mime how they do each activity. Sit in a circle and ask a volunteer to mime an activity. Ask others to guess and the one who guesses correctly has the next turn to mime.

4. What I'm good at

Talk to the chidren about learning new skills. Ask them to think about the process of learning this. Did they wake up one morning and find they could do it or did they have to learn? Who and what helped?

I am good at reading. My teacher and Jimmy helped me. It took a long time to learn but now I read to my sister. It makes me feel good.

Pass the sentence

Ask the children to think of one thing that they are good at and how they learned to do this thing.

'I am good at ... and I learned to do it by ...'

Vote with your feet

Choose six activities they mentioned; choose a place for children to stand to show which they are best at. Count them and make a chart of the results.

Imagine it/Stand and tell

Ask children to close their eyes and think of how they would feel if they couldn't do this thing that they are good at. What would they do? Would they start to learn it now and who would they ask to help?

Ask volunteers to say what they would do.

Pass the sentence

Talk about how they feel when they are doing this thing.

'I feel ... when I am ...'

Talk about how they felt when they were learning to do it.

'I felt ... when I was learning to ...'

Haiku

Read the haiku on the facing page. Ask the children to compose, write out and illustrate one haiku about the thing they are really good at.

Further work

Ask the children to think about all the things they are good at and to draw on one sheet of paper several little pictures of themselves doing this thing, each with a speech bubble telling what they are doing and how they are feeling.

5. Empathy

Explain to the children what the word 'empathy' means. It's all about thinking about other peoples' feelings and trying hard to understand how they are feeling.

Tell a story

> Ricky didn't like school. He wasn't very good at his work and even though he tried hard to make friends no one seemed to want to play with him. Tom was not really an unkind boy but he tried to make fun of Ricky's work by saying unkind things in the playground about Ricky and his work.

Ask the children to think about Ricky's feelings and what they could do if he were at their school.

Pass the sentence

> 'If I were Ricky I would feel ...'

> 'I could help Ricky by ...'

If I were Ricky, I would feel that no one liked me.

Jot down

Make a list of Ricky's feelings and the children's suggestions of how they could help him.

Hands-up session – in Ricky's shoes

Talk about what they could do if they were Ricky. What advice would they give to him about body language and being positive? Ask the children to raise their hand it they have suggestions to offer.

Haiku

Read this haiku and talk again about how you can feel empathy for other people. Ask the children to help you write a class haiku about empathy.

> **Empathy**
> Get inside their shoes!
> Can you get inside their skin?
> Think of how they feel.

Further work

Ask the children to think of a happy ending to Ricky's story and to draw a picture of themselves with Ricky. Help them to write a few words in a speech bubble about the happy ending.

5. Empathy

Before coming to the circle write the word 'empathy' on the board and give the children five minutes to work in their groups to use books to try to find out what it means.

Stand and tell

In the circle ask a spokesperson from each group to tell their meaning of the word. Ask a volunteer to suggest other words from this root word, such as empathetic, empathise, empathising. Write these on the board. Ask volunteers to suggest a sentence using one of these words.

Empathy means:

sharing their feelings
identifying with
having rapport
sympathising
understanding
responding to
relating to
knowing how they feel
being in their place.

Jot down

Make a list of what they say, even if it is not correct. Then read a dictionary definition and explain what it means. Which group said it best? Can they re-write one new definition of the word?

Tell a story

Ask each group to work together for five minutes to compose a story about someone feeling empathy for someone else. Ask them to write down key words from the story so that they will remember it.

Stand and tell

Ask a spokesperson from each group to tell their story. Discuss each story after it has been told. Is each story a good example of someone showing empathy? Which is the best example?

Haiku

Read the haiku on the facing page and ask the children to think of the stories they have just listened to and to work in pairs to write their own haiku about empathy.

Further work

Ask the children to think about how they can empathise with someone they like very much, then someone they don't like. What kinds of things can they do? Without using names, ask them to write about what they can do and say.

6. Working together

Explain that it is very important for people to work together. Remind the children of the story of the little red hen and how she did all the work with her little chicks and at the end the duck and the pig wanted to eat the bread but that she said 'No', and she and her little chicks ate it.

If they had all helped the little red hen, they could all eat the bread.

Imagine it

Ask the children to close their eyes and imagine what would have happened if the duck and the pig had helped the little red hen. Would it have made things better or worse? What would have happened if the hen had let the lazy duck and pig eat the bread too? Do they think that the little red hen was teaching the duck and pig a lesson here? What is the lesson?

Pass the sentence

'If they had all helped ...'

Stand and show

Ask the children to go to their places and draw a picture of the little red hen, her chicks, the duck and the pig all working together. Help them to write a sentence about their picture.

Ask the children to bring their pictures to the circle and to stand and show them to the rest of the class.

Haiku

Read this haiku with the children and talk about co-operating and helping each other. Ask them to help you write a class haiku about working together.

> **Working together**
> We help each other.
> Co-operation is good,
> Then we all do well.

Further work

Ask the children to think of other stories or rhymes where people worked together. Can they help you to make a collection of these? For example, Jack and Jill who walked up the hill together, all the king's horses and men in 'The Grand Old Duke of York', 'The Owl and the Pussycat.'

6. Working together

Talk to the children about co-operation and co-operating. Explain that when people work together the work gets done more quickly and people are happier. Explain the saying, 'Many hands make light work'.

Imagine it

Ask the children to imagine a family where everyone except the Mum was lazy and wouldn't help. Mum had to do all the work. How would she feel? What would happen if everyone helped?

Pass the sentence

'If I helped mum I think she would feel ...'

'If everyone helped ...'

Which way of helping do they think is the best?

If everyone helped, the work would soon be done and they could enjoy themselves.

Stand and tell

Ask volunteers to tell you something that they do to help at home and make a list of these.

Ask volunteers to tell you something they do at school to help. Make a second list. Talk about both lists.

Touch your ...

Ask the children to think about co-operating at school, or not. Ask them to:

- touch their nose if they think co-operating at school is a good thing
- touch one ear if they think helping a friend is a good thing
- wriggle their shoulders if they think helping at home is a good thing.

Haiku

Read the haiku from the facing page to the children. Ask them to compose haiku about working together and co-operating.

Further work

Ask the children to write and illustrate a story about someone who was not co-operative at first but who learned that working together is a good thing. Share these stories in Circle Time.

Let's celebrate self-esteem!

Work together
Play together
We'll all feel good
For ever and ever.

In Circle Time talk with the children about all the work they have done about self-esteem. Praise their illustrations and writing. Praise them for their work and for their learning.

Pass the sentence

Ask the children to tell you what they learned about using people's names.

'I've learned that ...'

Ask them to tell you what they have learned about everyone being special.

'I've learned that ...'

Ask them to tell you what they have learned about working together.

'I've learned that ...'

Extension activities

Remind the children about body language and ask them to show you how they look when they feel positive and happy. Ask them to think of how they can help someone who doesn't feel good about himself. What can they say and do to help this person?

Ask the children to work in groups to write a poem about what you can do if you're feeling sad to make yourself feel better.

Ask the children to think about helping other people to feel good about themselves. What can they do?

Remind the children about co-operating and working together. Can they write a slogan about this? For

A feeling good poem

When I'm feeling sad
or when things are going wronq
I stand up very, very tall
and sing a happy song.

I count up all the good thi
I count up what I'm good at
I remember how I'm special
and think of all my friends.

Stand up tall
Smile and say
Today will be
a very good day.

example, 'Work together, play together, that's the way to stay together'. Ask them to write this out on the computer and to illustrate it for a wall display.

Theme 5 Keeping healthy

1. A happy, healthy person
2. We need to exercise
3. Sleep and rest
4. Keeping clean
5. Healthy eating
6. Emotional health.

Explain to the children exactly what a haiku is.
They don't have to abide by the 5-7-5 rule when they compose their own.

The following haiku can be used in this section:

A haiku is a:
Poem in three lines
Five syllables, then seven
Five again. No rhyme.

A happy, healthy person	Keeping clean
If you are healthy You should be happy as well. Health and happiness.	Bath, shower and brush That is what we need to do, Bodies, face and hair.
We need to exercise Running and jumping Are ways of keeping healthy. Active and happy.	**Healthy eating** We are what we eat. Not all food is good for us. Some is just for treats.
Sleep and rest Sleep is important. It helps our bodies to grow. Our brains need to rest.	**Emotional health** Love and happiness Help to make our lives complete. Care and be cared for.

1. A happy, healthy person

I think healthy means you are not often ill.

Pass the sentence

Ask the children if they can tell you what 'healthy' means.

'I think healthy means ...'

Jot down

Make a list of key words they use. Have they given words such as fit, well, hearty, strong, fine, glowing, thriving? Look at each of the words in turn and say 'Can you be healthy if you are not fit, strong, well?' etc. Talk about people who are ill in some way but are still healthy – e.g. people in a wheelchair, with a broken a bone, are diabetic, have asthma.

Stand and show

Ask the children to go to their places and draw a picture of a healthy person. Ask them to draw around their picture all the things that the person has and all the things their person does to be healthy and to keep healthy.

As the children show their pictures to the group, make a list of all the things they say their person has and does to keep healthy. How many of their drawings show the person smiling?

Vote with your feet

Look at your list and ask the children to help you to choose the most important six things to write on the board. Ask the children to look at the list and choose which, for them, is the most important thing on your list. Select a place in the room for each word and ask the children to vote with their feet and to count themselves. Write these numbers alongside the word.

Haiku

Read this haiku with the children and talk about how they can keep themselves healthy. Ask them to help you write a class haiku about being healthy.

> **A happy, healthy person**
> If you are healthy
> You should be happy as well.
> Health and happiness.

Further work

Ask each child to remember their vote for the best thing for them to keep themselves healthy and to draw a picture of them doing this thing. Make a display of all these healthy drawings under an appropriate title – e.g. 'How we like to keep healthy'.

1. A happy, healthy person

Talk about being healthy and the things you can do to be and stay healthy. Ask the children to think of their part in staying healthy and to think of one thing they can do.

Stand, tell and sit down quickly

Ask the children to tell you this one thing and make a list of what they say, putting a tick alongside any repeats.

Next ask the children to decide whether these people can be healthy and to say yes or no:

- people who have asthma
- people who are diabetic
- people who have broken a leg
- people who have Down's syndrome.

Ask volunteers to justify their response.

> To be healthy, you can:
>
> jump and run
> eat fruit
> drink water
> stay out of the sun
> go to bed on time
> wash yourself
> clean your teeth
> have showers
> eat vegetables
> play outside.

Pass the sentence

Talk about being happy as part of being healthy and that being a happy person shows that you have good mental health – that is, your brain and head are healthy if you are happy.

'I think happy people are ...'

Haiku

Read the haiku from the facing page to the children. Ask them each to compose a haiku about either being healthy or being happy or both. Remind them of the list of words and their responses to people who have a health condition.

Further work

Ask each child to fold a paper into six sections and to draw themselves doing something in each section that shows they are trying to keep themselves healthy. Ask them to write what each thing is and how it will make and keep them healthy. Remind them that being happy and keeping safe are also important parts of being and staying healthy.

2. We need to exercise

Pass the sentence

Tell the children that exercise is an important part of keeping healthy and that you want to find out if they know what exercise is.

'I think exercise is ...'

I think exercise is playing football.

Stand, tell and sit down quickly

Ask the children to think of one thing they have done today that is exercise and to tell the group, using just one word.

Jot down

Make a list of all the different things that the children said. Write this on the board and ask if they can add anything else to the list.

Stand and tell

Ask volunteers to say how exercise keeps them healthy or what would happen if they did not do any exercise at all. After each contribution see if any of the others can add something to help you build up a picture of exercise as a bone-strengthening and heart-strengthening part of life.

Pass the sentence

Talk about how we look and feel after we have been exercising; we have a healthy glow and a good feeling inside us. Ask the children to tell you their favourite kind of exercising.

'My best kind of exercise is ...'

Haiku

Read this haiku and remind the children of different kinds of exercise. Ask them to help you write a class haiku about exercise as a part of keeping healthy.

> **We need to exercise**
> Running and jumping
> Are ways of keeping healthy.
> Active and happy.

Further work

Ask the children to draw themselves with a friend doing some kind of exercise together. Ask them to suggest a caption for their picture and help them to write it. Display these with some of the haiku under the heading 'We need to exercise'.

2. We need to exercise

Pass the sentence

Ask the children to think of all the kinds of exercise that they and other people do and to think about why people exercise.

'I think people exercise because ...'

Talk about the different parts of the body that benefit from exercise; about aerobic exercise and about weight-bearing exercise.

Pass the sentence

Talk about what could happen to our bodies if we didn't exercise.

'If we didn't exercise, we ...'

Jot down

Make a list of all the things the children say about not doing exercise.

> I think people exercise because ...
>
> they enjoy it
> it's good for you
> it helps you to grow
> it's good for health
> it makes them feel good
> it's a kind of play
> you choose to do it
> it's like a game
> we all like sports
> they like PE.

Stand and tell

Ask volunteers to tell the group their favourite kind of exercise – the exercise they would keep doing If they had the choice. Make a list of all these kinds of exercise.

Vote with your feet

Ask the group to vote on which kind of exercise they like doing best. Write down the results of this with the number of voters in each category. Ask the children to work in pairs to make a chart of these findings and to write a short explanation of their chart and how they got the results for it.

Haiku

Read the haiku from the facing page to the children. Remind them of the different kinds of exercise on the list and ask them each to compose a haiku about exercise.

Further work

Ask the children to talk to their families about the kinds of exercise they do. As them to jot down these kinds of exercises and how often their families do them. Ask volunteers to talk about this tomorrow in Circle Time.

3. Sleep and rest

Stand and tell

Talk to the children about the importance of sleep and rest. What do they think happens when they rest? What happens when we sleep? Ask volunteers to give responses to the two questions.

If we don't sleep...

we are tired
we can't do our work
we get grumpy
we keep falling asleep
we don't grow well
we look pale and ill
we can't exercise.

Pass the sentence

Ask the children to think about what happens if they don't get enough sleep.

'If we don't sleep ...'

Stand and tell

Talk about bedtime routine and ask children to tell about theirs – e.g. do they bath or shower, do they have a story, do they sleep in their own room, have they a special bedtime?

Hands-up session – sleepovers

Talk about when children go on sleepovers and ask them to think about how much sleep they get then. Do they stay awake for a long time? What kinds of things do they do? Ask the children to raise their hand if they have suggestions to make.

Pass the sentence

'When I went on a sleepover ...'

Haiku

Read this haiku about sleep and rest and ask the children to help you write two class haiku – one about sleep and one about rest.

Sleep and rest
Sleep is important.
It helps our bodies to grow.
Our brains need to rest.

Further work

Ask the children to think about how many hours' sleep they have each night and how many hours other people have. Can they come to an agreement about the hours a baby needs, a teenager, their parents or carers? Ask them to draw pictures of these different-aged people asleep and to write the number of hours they think these people need to sleep so that they will be bright and alert each day. Ask them to take these home to see if their families agree.

3. Sleep and rest

Talk to the children about sleep and rest – can anyone tell you the difference? Do they know that it is very important that all people have enough sleep? Do they know that we grow when we are asleep and that children who do not get enough sleep may not be as tall and heavy as those who do?

Our sleep times

4 say 11 hours
8 say 10 hours
15 say 9 hours
3 say 8 hours.

Stand, tell and sit down quickly

Ask the children to think of how many hours' sleep they normally get on a school day. Ask them to tell you, giving just the number of hours.

Jot down

Make a list of these hours, ticking the number when you get a similar response. Make a quick chart on the board using these numbers. Are the children surprised at their differing sleep patterns?

Stand, tell and sit down quickly

Ask the children to tell, in one word, the time they go to bed.

Pass the sentence

Talk about the need for sleep and what happens if children don't get enough sleep. What suffers?

'If I don't get enough sleep ...'

Haiku

Read the haiku from the facing page to the children. Ask them to work in pairs to compose two haiku – one about getting enough sleep and one about not getting enough.

Further work

Ask all the children to vote with their feet and stand in a place to denote their normal bedtime. Ask each group to make a chart about bedtimes and to make this the centre of a display with each child writing about their own bedtime and getting-up routine. Ask them to put their finished display on their group table and ask other groups to go around the classroom looking at them. Can they all vote on one to display on the classroom wall?

4. Keeping clean

Talk to the children about babies and how their carers keep them clean. Explain that babies need to be kept really clean, especially when they wear nappies.

Stand and tell

Ask any of the children who have a baby at home to explain the keeping clean routine that the grown-ups use for their baby.

My bathtime

My mum runs the bath and I get in and wash myself. Then she washes me a bit more and watches me clean my teeth.

Pass the sentence

Ask the children to think about their own bathtime and whether their parents bath them or whether they do part or all of it for themselves.

'At my bath time, I ...'

Hands-up session

Talk about the difference between having a bath or shower and ask children to raise a hand if they have a bath, then raise it if they have a shower. Note these numbers. Ask the children which they think is best for them and for the water company. How can they be careful with water?

Stand, tell and sit down quickly

Talk about hair washing and ask if any of them like to have their hair washed. Make this into a 'yes' 'no' session to get an idea of who does and who doesn't. Ask volunteers to give their reasons why they like or don't like having their hair washed. What could happen if they didn't have it washed?

Haiku

Read this haiku about keeping clean and ask the children to help you write two class haiku – one about baths and one about showers.

> **Keeping clean**
> Bath, shower and brush
> That is what we need to do,
> Bodies, face and hair.

Further work

Talk about washing hands, especially before eating and after doing something dirty. Explain that hand washing takes time. They should be able to sing 'Happy birthday to you' all the way through while doing it. Practise this!

4. Keeping clean

Pass the sentence

Talk to the children about keeping themselves clean and ask them to think about why this is important.

  'It's important to keep clean because ...'

Jot down

Make a list of their reasons.

It's important to keep clean because ...

there are germs
you could get ill
you might eat dirt
you would smell
you'd look horrid
no one would like you
you'd have no friends
you'd look a mess
your skin would go funny.

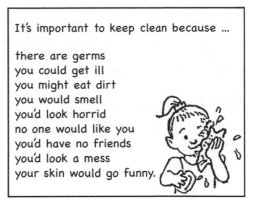

Imagine it

Talk to the children about life long ago when people did not have bathrooms and rarely washed. Explain that they wore perfume and carried posies sometimes to make them smell better. Talk about life, not all that long ago, when a family might have a zinc bath to put in front of the fire once a week and fill with water from kettles. Often the cleanest person bathed first and everyone used the same water.

Pass the sentence

Talk about today when most people have bathrooms and showers. Which do they think is best?

  'I like to have a bath [or shower] because ...'

Haiku

Read the haiku from the facing page to the children. Explain that the word 'hygiene' means things being really clean so that no germs or bacteria are present. In hospitals they are very careful about hygiene. Explain that it is important to wash hands before eating so that we are hygienic and don't eat dirt or germs with our food. (See facing page for how to wash hands.) Ask the children to compose a haiku about hygiene.

Further work

Ask the children to write a story about a child who lived long ago who was transported into today's time. What would they think about hygiene, washing machines, bathrooms, showers, hairdressers, launderettes, carwashes, etc.

5. Healthy eating

Before Circle Time ask the children to draw two pictures – one of some food they really like to eat and the other of a food that they know is not really so healthy.

I like to eat crisps. A healthy food is an apple.

Stand and show

As the children show their pictures, make two quick lists of both kinds of foods on the board – healthy foods, not so healthy foods. Read through the list of the things they like, talking about each one. Are there any healthy foods in this list? If so, draw an arrow to the list of healthy foods. Read through the list of foods they say are healthy; are there any that are not so healthy? If so, draw an arrow to the other list.

Pass the sentence

Talk about foods that are for treats – foods that are not so healthy, but that we like to have on certain occasions. Explain that most people like these foods but that it would not be good for them to eat them all the time.

  'A treat food I like is ...'

Make a third list alongside the other two, headed 'Treats', and ask the children if they could move some of the foods from the 'not so healthy' list into the 'treats' list. If they mention a really healthy food as a treat food, talk about this and add it to the healthy list.

Do the same activity with drinks, explaining at the end that water is best.

Haiku

Read this haiku about healthy eating. Help the children to learn it and then to compose a healthy eating haiku.

> **Healthy eating**
> We are what we eat
> Not all food is good for us.
> Some is just for treats.

Further work

Duplicate a copy of the above haiku for each child on a large piece of paper and ask them to draw healthy foods around the words. Ask them to draw a box at the bottom of the paper labelled 'treats' and to draw some treat foods inside the box.

5. Healthy eating

Pass the sentence

Ask the children to think of one healthy drink and one healthy food.

> 'I think a healthy drink is ...'

I think a healthy food is bread.

I think a healthy drink is milk.

Jot down

Jot down the drinks they mention and when they've all had a turn, go through the list and ask them to help you draw a ring around the ones that are really healthy. Have they included water?

Do the same activity with foods: 'I think a healthy food is ...' Make a second list.

Stand, tell and sit down quickly

Talk about 'five a day' and explain that we now think that eating five fruits or vegetables a day is good for our health. Go around the circle asking the children to raise their hand and tell you one fruit; do the activity again about vegetables.

Hands-up session

Look at your original lists of healthy foods. Are there any fruits and vegetables there? If so, draw a ring around these. Ask volunteers to raise their hands and tell you fruits and vegetables that you can add on to the bottom of the list.

Haiku

Read the haiku on the facing page. Ask the children to write two more haiku – one about healthy foods, the other about healthy drinks. Vote on the best to display.

Further work

Ask the children to bring into school labels or empty cans and bottles of drink. In Circle Time read the labels to the children, looking for sugars and caffeine. Talk about these as not being good for our health and try to identify those with the least sugar and caffeine. Working in groups ask them to make a chart showing the sugar content of all the drinks in order – least sugar at the top of the list. Explain that the healthiest drink of all is water.

6. Emotional health

Remind the children that it is important to keep our bodies healthy. Explain, however, that this is not enough and that we must keep our minds healthy too. We do this by caring for and thinking of other people and having other people care for and love us.

A person who loves and cares for me is my sister.

Pass the sentence

Ask the children to think of someone at home who loves or cares for them.

'A person who loves and cares for me is ...'

Ask the children to think about how they would feel if this person were not here any more.

'I would feel ...'

Jot down

Make a list of these 'feelings' words. Read out the words and talk about them.

Stand, tell and sit down quickly

Ask the children to think of someone they really care about who is not in the class and to say this person's name.

Pass the sentence

Talk about the kinds of things we do to care for other people – how do we show them that we care?

'I show I care when I ...'

Haiku

Read this haiku about emotional health. Ask the children to help you write two more haiku – one about someone who cares for you and the other about caring for others.

> **Emotional health**
> Love and happiness
> Help to make our lives complete.
> Care and be cared for.

Further work

Ask the children to draw all the people and pets in their family and to draw themselves doing things that show they care for these people and pets. Help them to write about their pictures. Ask them to take them home to share with their families.

6. Emotional health

Stand and tell

Ask the children if they can think of what 'emotional health' or 'mental health' might mean.

Jot down

Make a list of what they say. If they have not got it quite right, explain that this kind of health is to do with feeling good about yourself, caring about other people, feeling that other people care about you and being able to cope with various feelings in a positive way. Read through the list and help the children to understand the importance of positive emotional health.

Emotional health
feel good about self
a positive outlook
care for people
feel empathy
think before you act
in charge of feelings
careful decisions
cope with pain
good communication
being optimistic
healthy attitude
feel secure

Imagine it/Pass the sentence

Ask the children to close their eyes and think about all aspects of emotional health. Then ask them to pass these sentences:

'I show I think of other people when I ...'
'I know people care for me when ...'
'I show I am in charge of my feelings when ...'

Touch your ...

Ask the children to think about how positive they feel about themselves.

- 'Touch your nose if you think you usually feel good about yourself.'
- 'Raise a thumb if you think you can control what you do when you get angry.'
- 'Put a thumb down if you let your feelings get out of control quite often.'
- 'Give a big smile if you think you are a good friend.'
- 'Touch your knees if you think you are good at talking and listening to people.'

Haiku

Read the haiku on the facing page and talk about it. Ask them to write a haiku using the list they made about emotional health.

Further work

Ask the children to work in pairs to write the first part of a story about someone who got really angry with a friend. Ask them to write two endings, one where their character was in control of their feelings and resolved the situation, the other where they lost control.

Let's celebrate keeping healthy!

In Circle Time talk with the children about all the work they have done about keeping themselves healthy. Praise their drawings and writing. Praise them for their work and for their learning.

Pass the sentence

Ask the children to tell you what they learned about exercise.

> 'I've learned that ...'

Ask them to tell you what they have learned about sleep and rest.

> 'I've learned that ...'

Ask them to tell you what they have learned about keeping clean.

> 'I've learned that ...'

Extension activities

Remind them about healthy eating and 'five a day'. Ask children to work in pairs and identify the ingredients of a healthy meal. Ask them to draw a place setting with a dinner plate and pudding plate and to draw the items on the plates that they think would make a good, healthy main meal. On another piece of paper ask them to draw in the kinds of treats they like and to write how often they think they should eat these treats.

Ask the class to work in groups to write a rap, poem or song about keeping healthy. Ask them to vote for the best one and to write this on the computer with good graphics to display.

Keeping healthy rap

Time to keep healthy
Treat your body well
What shall we eat then?
Does everybody know?
Not many treats and five a day!
Healthy, healthy, that's the way to go.

How shall we keep clean?
Showers and baths
Teeth clean, shiny hair
Skin clean and fresh
Don't forget to hand wash
Keep germs away
Healthy, healthy, that's how we'll stay.

We all need sound sleep
to be alert all day
Exercise to help us grow
well in every way.
Feel good about ourselves
that's self-esteem
Manage our feelings
Care for our friends
That'll keep us healthy
Right till the end.

Theme 6 Feelings and Persuasion

1. Feeling good

2. Feelings we share

3. How can we tell how people are feeling?

4. Feelings change

5. Feeling afraid – what can we do?

6. Good persuasion

7. Bad persuasion

8. Saying 'no' to bad persuasion.

I am feeling good today

Explain to the children exactly what a haiku is. They don't have to abide by the 5-7-5 rule when they compose their own.

> **A haiku is a:**
> Poem in three lines
> Five syllables, then seven
> Five again. No rhyme.

The following haiku can be used in this section:

Feeling good	**Feeling afraid – what can we do?**
When I am happy	When I'm really scared
Excited, glad and jolly	And afraid of something bad
Then I'm feeling good.	I think of good things.
Feelings we share	**Good persuasion**
Scared, cross or worried,	People persuade us
We all feel like this at times.	To do good and helpful things.
We are not alone.	That's good persuasion.
How can we tell how people are feeling?	**Bad persuasion**
We can read faces	If we know it's wrong,
And look at body language.	We mustn't be persuaded.
These show how they feel.	Someone will get hurt.
Feelings change	**Saying 'no' to bad persuasion**
Sometimes I feel sad	You have to say 'no'
Then I try to cheer me up	Or you will be in trouble.
Thinking of good things.	Say 'no' loud and clear.

1. Feeling good

Tell the children that today you want them to think about when they feel really good and happy.

Pass the face

Tell the children to show by their face how they feel when they are feeling good and happy. Pass the face around the circle.

Pass the sentence

Now ask them to think of some of the things that make them feel really good.

'I feel really good when ...'

List key words that they say and when all have had their turn read out your list.

You may find that the children's responses can be put into several categories such as 'something I have' (e.g. a present or toy), 'something I have done' (e.g. an achievement such as finishing a book), 'something someone has done for or to me' (e.g. made me laugh when I felt sad). Talk about the different kinds of things that make us feel good.

Stand, tell and sit down quickly

Now ask the children to think of something they can do to make someone in their family feel good. Ask them to think of one person they want to make feel good and to say that person's name.

Pass the sentence

How do the children feel when they make someone else feel good?

'When I make someone feel good it makes me feel ...'

List these 'feelings' words – e.g. happy, glad, surprised, pleased, excited. Can they add more?

We feel
happy
good
glad
lovely
pleased.

Haiku

Read this haiku to the children and talk about how you look when you're feeling good. Ask them to give you words about feeling good to help to compose one or more class haiku. Ask older children to work individually to compose, write out and illustrate their own haiku.

> **Feeling good**
> When I am happy
> Excited, glad and jolly
> Then I'm feeling good.

Further work

Ask the children to draw themselves making someone else feel good. Label their drawings or use speech bubbles to show what they are saying. Display these near some of the haiku.

1. Feeling good

Pass the face

Ask the children to think of something they have done recently that made them feel good about themselves.

Ask them to pass the kind of face they have when they are feeling good.

Stand, tell and sit down quickly/Change places

Ask the children to think of a word or phrase that they could use instead of 'feeling good'. Ask those who repeat a word or phrase to change places with the last person who said it. Make a list of key words; read out your list.

Pass the sentence

Ask the children to tell one thing that makes them feel good about themselves.

'I feel good when I ...' or 'I feel good ...'

Pass the sentence

Ask the children to think of something they could do to make someone at school feel good today without saying anyone's name.

'To make someone feel good I could ...'

'Feeling good' words
Happy, good, glad, lovely friendly, thoughtful helped, kindly caring, excited better, loving wonderful.

Haiku

Read and talk about the haiku on the facing page. Ask the children to suggest words they could use instead of 'feeling good' and list these. Ask them to work in pairs to compose, write and illustrate two haiku, using at least two of the 'feeling good' words from the list, or their own.

Further work

Ask the children to put the list of words in some kind of order – alphabetical or families. Ask the children to illustrate some of these words and use these to make a chart of these 'feeling good' words.

In groups ask the children to discuss something that made their group feel good and to write and draw about what happened and how it made them feel.

2. Feelings we share

Pass the face

Ask the children to think of times when they were not feeling good and how they looked then. Ask them to make that face and pass this face around the circle.

| **Feelings we share** |
| Scared, cross or worried, |
| We all feel like this at times. |
| We are not alone. |

Pass the sentence

Ask the children to think about something that made them feel not so good.

'This is how I felt when ...'

If you can, suggest the word that would name that feeling and say it to the group – e.g. 'So you felt *worried* when you dropped the glass.'

List these feelings on the board. When all the children have had their turn, read out your list and talk about these feelings.

Stand up if ...

Ask the children to stand up if they shared the same feelings – e.g. 'If you told me that you felt sad [or silly, worried or scared], stand up.'

Ask the children to help to count the number of standing children and add that number to the list you made. Remind the children that we all have these feelings from time to time – we need to recognise these feelings in other people so that we can know how they are feeling.

Haiku

Read this haiku to the children. Read again the list of 'feelings' words and ask which would be good to use in a haiku about feelings they share. Draw a coloured ring around those words. Use some of them to help to compose one or more class haiku. Ask older children to work individually to compose, write out and illustrate their own haiku.

| **Feelings we share** |
| We told about feeling sad (10). |
| We told about feeling worried (3). |
| We told about feeling scared (6). |

Further work

Show the children how to make drawn faces show expression – by the shape of the mouth or eyes. Ask them to draw faces to show different expressions. Label these faces, perhaps grouping them together to make a class collage. Use the list of 'feelings' words for reading practice or spelling aids.

2. Feelings we share

Tell a story

Sam was trying hard to help his mum to tidy the table. There was a puzzle on the table which Sam's brother Tom had nearly finished. Sam carried the box with the puzzle very carefully but he didn't notice the kitten was near his feet. Just as he got to the cupboard, he tripped over the kitten and fell over. Sam's fingers were hurting where they hit the cupboard and the puzzle was spoilt.

Pass the face

Ask the children to think about how the people in the story felt and to show by their face how each character, including the kitten, felt. Ask them to choose someone from the story, make the appropriate face and say how they felt.

I think the kitten would have looked like this.

'They would feel ...'

Stand and tell

Talk to the children about the importance of recognising how other people are feeling. Ask for volunteers to show and say how they think:

- Mum would have looked and felt ... if she had spoiled the puzzle
- Tom would have looked and felt ... if he had spoiled the puzzle himself
- the kitten would have looked and felt ... if it had fallen over on its own.

Pass the sentence

Can they tell you what they could do to help people to feel better?

'To make someone feel better you could ...'

Haiku

Read and talk about the haiku on the facing page. Ask the children to list 'feelings' words under two headings – good feelings, bad feelings. Ask them to work in pairs and use these to write two haiku – one about feeling good, the other about feeling bad.

Further work

Talk about hurting people's feelings and ask the children to think of a time when they hurt someone's feelings by accident. Ask them to draw a picture and write a sentence about it. Ask older children to write about how they felt when this happened and what they did to try to make it better.

3. How can we tell how people are feeling?

Tell a story

Chris was playing with friends in the playground. Sanjay knocked Chris down. Chris sat there for a minute trying to think how it felt. Sally came and helped Chris up but Anwar thought Chris looked funny sitting there and began to laugh.

Ask the children to think about how Chris, Sanjay, Sally and Anwar were feeling. Ask how we could tell how they were feeling. Ask them to show by their face or body how each child might have felt.

Stand and tell

Divide the group or circle into four parts and ask the children in the first part to pretend they were Chris, to show everyone how he would have felt.

'I think Chris would have looked and felt like this . . .'

Ask the next quarter of children to think of Sanjay and so on until all the children have had their turn.

Stand up if ...

Ask the children to stand up
- if they have fallen and people have laughed at them
- if they have laughed at someone when they got hurt.

Stand and mime

Ask a volunteer to stand up, be one of the children in the story and mime how they felt. Ask the rest to put up hands if they can guess who the person is. The correct person is next to have a turn.

Haiku

Read this haiku to the children. Talk about reading faces and body language. Ask for words that children could use in a haiku and help younger children to compose a class haiku. Ask older children to compose, write out and illustrate their own haiku.

> **How can we tell how people are feeling?**
> We can read faces
> And look at body language.
> These show how they feel.

Further work

Display a selection of the haiku. Ask the children to help to make a class picture of the story. Ask them to say what they think happened next and write their words in a speech bubble around it.

3. How can we tell how people are feeling?

Ask the children to think about how people show how they are feeling. Explain that we show our feelings not only by our face but also by our body language. Demonstrate to the children how the body and face can look when feeling sad, happy, excited.

Pass the face/pose

Play this game around the group or circle, with children standing up to show by faces and bodies emotions such as: joy, excitement, fear, worry, happiness, love, wonder. (The teacher chooses the feeling or asks children to choose and say which feelings they are showing.)

Read the story of Chris, Sanjay, Sally and Anwar from the facing page.

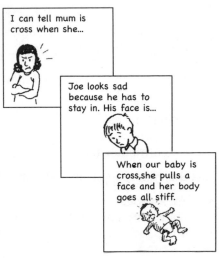

I can tell mum is cross when she...

Joe looks sad because he has to stay in. His face is...

When our baby is cross, she pulls a face and her body goes all stiff.

Question and answer

Divide the circle into four sections. Using a different name for each segment so that all four children's feelings are explored, ask each segment the first question. (The second format may be easier for some children.)

- 'How do you think Chris felt?' 'What made you think that?'
- 'I think Chris [or other name] felt ... because he was ...'

Haiku

Read and talk about the haiku on the facing page. Ask the children to suggest words that describe face or body expressions. Ask them to work in their groups with each child composing and illustrating one haiku, then mounting them to form a group display on a large piece of paper or card.

Further work

Explain to the children that adults call these feelings emotions. Ask them to choose one emotion and draw how people look when they feel like that.

Ask older children to choose one of the characters in the story. Ask them to draw the character, think of what could have happened next and to write a good ending.

4. Feelings change

Stand up if ...

Ask the children to think about how people are all the same.
Ask them to stand up if they have:

* two eyes
* hair
* two legs.

(Choose attributes that all children posses.)

Ask the children to stand up if they have:

* blue eyes
* long/short hair
* black/brown hair.

(Choose attributes that are fairly constant.)

I'm sad.

Ask the children to stand up if they have:

* black shoes
* a blue cardigan
* white socks
* a green jersey.

(Choose attributes that change.)

Pass the sentence

'I'm the same as you because I have ... [blue eyes, two ears, brown hair].'

Now ask the children to think of how their feelings change.

'Yesterday I felt ... but today I feel ...'

I'm not sad.

Haiku

Read this haiku to the children. Talk about how we don't always feel the same and that feelings change. Ask for words that children could use in a haiku and help younger children to compose a class haiku about changing feelings. Ask older children to work in pairs to compose, write out and illustrate two haiku – one where feelings change from good to bad and vice versa.

> **Feelings change**
> Sometimes I feel sad
> Then I try to cheer me up
> Thinking of good things.

Further work

Ask the children to draw two pictures of themselves – one where they are happy and one where they are not happy. Talk to the children about their pictures as you label them. Display some of the haiku with these pictures.

4. Feelings change

Ask the children to think of some time when they felt bad, sad, unhappy or miserable and what happened or what they did to make themselves feel better.

> **Making me feel better.**
> When Jim feels bad, he goes to read a book.
> When Sara feels miserable she watches TV.
> When Jo feels unhappy he goes out to play football.

> **Helping others to feel better.**
> You can...
> tell them a joke
> say you understand
> play with them
> take them out somewhere
> give them a hug
> ask them to choose what to do.

Pass the sentence

'When I feel sad, I ...'

Make a list of what the children say and when all have had their turn, discuss ways to make ourselves feel better.

Hands-up session

Read each word on the list and ask the children:

- what the word means
- where else you can use it
- words that mean the same
- words that mean the opposite.

> I know you feel bad now, but let's have a game of football to cheer you up.

> You'll feel better tomorrow. Remember I'm your friend - come to my house and we'll play together.

Ask the children to think about using these words in other sentences and ask volunteers to tell the group.

Ask the children to think of the feelings of their friends and families. How can they help when these people feel sad or unhappy?

Pass the sentence

'When ... feels sad I can make them feel better by ...'

Haiku

Read and talk about the haiku on the facing page. Read through the 'feelings' word list again and ask the children to think which would be good to put in a haiku about helping sad people to feel better. Ask the children to write out their haiku and illustrate it.

Further work

Ask the children to draw themselves on some occasion when they felt unhappy and to write about what made them feel better. Make a collage of speech bubbles with advice to people who feel sad and display these near some haiku.

5. Feeling afraid – what can we do?

Tell the children of some occasion when you yourself felt afraid – noises in the dark, when you were alone – and what you did to overcome your fear.

Choose each of these fears in turn: the dark, fireworks, loud bangs, scary TV, and ask the children to stand up if they are afraid of it. Ask the children to think of what they do when they are afraid.

I am afraid of scary TV.
I close my eyes.

Pass the sentence

'When I'm scared I ...'

Reassure children that it is natural to feel afraid sometimes, and that this often helps us to take care of ourselves. (If there is something that you know your class is afraid of, perhaps you can talk about that here.)

Now choose one or more of the following to pass round the circle:

'If you are afraid of the dark, you can ...'
'If you are afraid of TV, you can ...'
'If you are afraid of blood, you can ...'
'If you are afraid of a person, you can ...'

When children express their fears they find that many of them are afraid of the same things – this alone can give confidence to overcome them.

Haiku

Read this haiku to the children. Talk about how we are all afraid of something and ask them to help you to make a list of their fears. Help the children to compose a class haiku about fears and what they do when they are afraid.

> **Feeling afraid – what can we do?**
> When I'm really scared
> And afraid of something bad
> I think of good things.

Further work

Look in the library for picture books to read about overcoming fears – such as:
A Lion at Bedtime by Debi Gliori (Scholastic, 1993).
Janine and the Carnival by Iolette Thomas (Mammoth, 1989).
Oliver and the Monsters by Tony Blundell (Viking Children's Books, 1993).
Dog Dottington by Diana Hendry (Walker Books, 1996).

5. Feeling afraid – what can we do?

Before coming to the circle ask the children to draw someone who is afraid and to write what this person is afraid of.

Stand and show

Ask all children to stand up in turn and show and talk about their picture. Ask if their fears fit into any categories. They may suggest fears that are real, fears that involve their own wrongdoing and fears that are fantasy and unlikely to happen.

Real fears	Doing wrong fears	Fantasy fears
falling out of bed getting into trouble breaking things people being cross.	getting found out after: taking things going to places out of bounds doing things they shouldn't.	getting beamed up by aliens swimming in shark filled waters getting hit by lightning.

Ask the children which fears are the most important to overcome.

Look at some of the examples the children gave and ask for solutions to these problems.

This is Sophie. She is afraid of monsters under the bed.

Pass the face

Ask the children, one at a time, to make a face that shows

- how they look and feel when they are afraid.
- how they look and feel when their fear goes away.

Pass each face around the circle.

Haiku

Read and talk about the haiku on the facing page. Ask the children for suggestions about what they can do to feel better when they are afraid. List these. Ask them to compose two haiku – one about things that scare them and the other about what they do to overcome their fears.

Further work

Ask the children to look again at the pictures they brought to the circle. Ask them to write alongside or on the back how this person they drew can overcome their fear. Read some stories about overcoming fear – look at the suggestions for younger children.

6. Good persuasion

Ask the children to tell you what they think persuasion is. With the youngest children you may have to give them the word and explain what it means. You could say that to persuade someone is to make them do something you want them to do – e.g. to tidy up, clean their teeth, put their coat on, help with the baby.

Pass the sentence

Choose one or both of the following:

'Good persuasion is when you persuade us to ...'

'It's good when my mum [or dad or family] persuades me to ...'

Talk about how people look and talk when they try to persuade us to do something good.

Good persuaders want us to...

pick up rubbish
keep things nice
help them
play with them
share things
lend things.

Please

Pass the sentence

Talk about who persuades us and what they encourage us to do.

'... persuades us to ...'

Pass the face

Pretend someone wants to persuade you to play their game – how will they look? Make the face and pass it around the circle.

Good persuaders ask us...

with a smile
in a nice voice
quietly
politely.

Stand and tell

Pretend someone wants to persuade you to do something. What will they say? How will they say it? Ask the children to take turns to stand up and tell you.

Haiku

Read this haiku to the children. Ask them to think of a time when they were persuaded to do something good and help them to use the ideas to compose several class haiku. Write these out and display them together under the heading 'Good persuasion'.

> **Good persuasion**
> People persuade us
> To do good and helpful things.
> That's good persuasion.

Further work

Ask the children to draw a grown-up at school persuading them to do something.

6. Good persuasion

Pass the face

Ask the children to think of a time when someone persuaded them to do something good for someone else – e.g. write a letter, make a gift, tidy the garden, help to wash the car. Ask the children to think of how the persuader looked and what they said. Show how they looked and pass the face around the circle.

Pass the sentence

What did they say and how did they say it? Ask them to pass the sentence using the right kind of voice.

'They said ...'

Ask how they felt when they were persuaded.

'When I did what the person persuaded me to do, I felt ...'

Stand and tell

Ask the children to think about times when people get together to try to persuade others to do something good – e.g. clear up litter, give money to charity, petition for a crossing, ask for help on a school or community project. Ask volunteers to stand and tell.

We brought tokens to school to help to buy computers.
We bought stickers to help save the whale.
We sponsored an animal in the wildlife park.
We had a sponsored walk to raise money for charity.
People went to the council to ask for a crossing.

Haiku

Read and talk about the haiku on the facing page. Remind them that it's about good persuasion. Ask them to think of an occasion when they were persuaded to do something good or useful and to compose a haiku about it. Ask them to write their haiku neatly and to mount and illustrate it. Choose some to display under the heading 'Good persuasion'.

Further work

Ask the children to work in groups to write a letter and to make a poster to persuade people to come to school to help. Ask each group to display their group poster and letter for everyone to see. Vote democratically to choose one or more to display in your classroom. Ask the children whether they think the poster and letter will persuade people to come and help.

7. Bad persuasion

Remind the children that there are two kinds of persuasion:

- when people ask you to do something that is good for you or others
- when people ask you to do something that is bad for you or others.

Ask the children to think of times when people have tried to persuade them to do something that they know is not right.

Pass the sentence

'It's not right when someone tries to persuade you to ...'

Pass the face/voice

What kind of face and voice does a bad persuader have? Show their face and say in their voice:

'Come on, let's do it; no one will know.'

Ask the children to think whether someone has ever tried to persuade them to do something they know is wrong.

It's OK

> **Bad persuaders try to make you**
> say they'll hurt you if you don't
> say they'll give you things if you do
> try to force you
> say no one will find out.

Stand, tell and sit down quickly

Ask the children to stand up and say 'yes' if someone has ever tried to persuade them to do something bad.

Remind the children that they must always say 'NO' to a bad persuader.

Haiku

Read this haiku to the children. Remind them that it's about bad persuasion. Ask them to help you make a list of things that a bad persuader might want them to do. Ask them to use ideas from this list to compose several class haiku about bad persuaders and bad persuasion.

> **Bad persuasion**
> If we know it's wrong,
> We mustn't be persuaded.
> Someone will get hurt.

Further work

Read or tell the story of *Little Red Riding Hood*. Talk to the children about the big bad wolf persuading her to do something that was bad for her. What should she have said to the wolf? Can they think of other stories when someone tried to persuade someone to do something wrong?

7. Bad persuasion

Stand up if ... Change places

Remind children that there is both good and bad persuasion.

Ask the children to stand up if someone has ever tried to persuade them to do something they know is wrong. Ask them to change places with anyone who is standing up.

Next ask the children to stand up if someone has ever tried to persuade them to do something they know is dangerous. Change places.

Pass the sentence/Change places

Ask them to think why people might try to persuade them to do something bad.

'They might want to persuade you to do something bad because ...'

Ask the children who repeat to change places with the person who said it last.

Jot down

Write what the children say and when they have all had their turn, talk about what they have said.

Haiku

Read and talk about the haiku on the facing page. Remind them that it's about bad persuasion. Ask them to think of something that a bad persuader might try to get them to do and to compose a haiku about it. Ask them to write their haiku neatly and to mount and illustrate it. Choose some to display under the heading 'Bad persuaders'.

Further work

Talk about the consequences of being persuaded to do something wrong or dangerous. Ask the children whose fault it is if they are persuaded to do that. (See the next page for ideas for helping children to say 'no'.)

Ask the children to write a story about someone who was tempted to do something they knew was wrong or dangerous.

People might want to persuade you to do something bad because:

it makes them feel good
they want to control you
they want you to do something they dare not do
they want you to share the blame.

8. Saying 'no' to bad persuasion

Remind the children that there is good persuasion as well as bad and that they should not be saying 'no' unless someone is trying to persuade them to do something they know is wrong or dangerous.

Stand up if ... Change places

Ask the children to stand up if a friend has ever tried to persuade them to do something they know is wrong or dangerous. Change places.

Pass the sentence

Ask the children to think of what they should *say* if someone tries to persuade them to do something that is wrong or dangerous.

> 'You could say ...'

Ask the children to think of what they should *do* if someone tries to persuade them to do something that is wrong or dangerous.

> 'You could ...'

> **Saying no**
> No, I'm not going to
> No, it's wrong
> No, it's not fair
> No, it's dangerous
> No, that's silly
> No, that could hurt someone.

If young children give inappropriate responses to both of the above, intervene – suggest better things to say and do. Jot down useful responses for later.

> **You could say:**
> No
> Go away
> I'll tell a grown-up
> I'm not going to.

What we really want the children to say is 'no' and what we want them to do is to go away quickly from the person trying to persuade them.

Stand up if ...

Ask those children who said 'say no' to stand up and ask them to say 'no' to the rest of the group. They must say it firmly and loudly.

Haiku

Read this haiku to the children. Talk about saying 'no' and how you say it. Help children to compose a 'say no' haiku for the classroom. Ask older children to compose, write out and illustrate their own 'say no' haiku. Display these.

> **Saying 'no' to bad**
> **persuasion**
> You have to say 'no'
> Or you will be in trouble.
> Say 'no' loud and clear.

Further work

Practise saying 'No' in a firm way. Repeat this sentence: 'No, I'm not going to.'

8. Saying 'no' to bad persuasion

Remind children that there are two kinds of persuasion and that they should always say 'no' to persuasion if it means doing or saying something wrong, dangerous or hurtful.

Pass the sentence/Change places

NO!

'Bad persuasion is when someone tries to make you ...'

Ask children who repeat a word or phrase to change places.

Tell children that it is sometimes difficult to resist persuasion. The best way is to start their sentence with 'No'.

> **Ways to say 'no'**
>
> Look them in the eye
> Stand straight and tall
> Take a deep breath
> Start with 'No'
>
> You don't need to give a reason – just say
> 'it's wrong'
> 'it's dangerous'
> 'someone could get hurt'.

Pass the sentence

Ask the children to think of one example from the 'pass the sentence' above and to think of what they would say if someone tried to persuade them to do that.

'No I won't, because ...'

Stand and tell/Jot down

Ask the children to think how they will say 'no' – How will it sound? How will their face look? How will their body look?

Ask the children to say 'no'. Make sure they do this in a forceful way.
Jot down anything appropriate that the children tell you about ways to say 'no' and include their responses in a chart for children to read and remember.

Haiku

Read and talk about the haiku on the facing page. Remind them that it's about saying 'no'. Ask them to work in groups to compose at least one haiku. Ask them to write it neatly and to mount and illustrate it. Choose some to display under the heading 'Say no to bad persuasion'.

Further work

Use drama to explore ways of saying 'no' to a partner.

Ask the children to choose one of the 'ways to say no' and to illustrate this.

Use some of their pictures to illustrate your chart.

Let's celebrate feelings and persuasion!

In Circle Time talk with the children about all the work they have done about feelings and persuasion. Admire the illustrations and the writing. Praise them for their work and for their learning.

Pass the sentence

Ask the children to tell you what they have learned about feelings.

'I know that feelings ...'

Ask the children to think about how to deal with sad feelings.

'When I am feeling down, I ...'

Ask the children to tell you what they have learned about good and bad persuasion.

'I know that good persuasion is ...'
'I know that bad persuasion is ...'

Ask the children what they know about saying 'no'.

'You have to say 'no' like this...'

Extension activities

Help them to write a class poem or song about feelings.

Use a drama session to ask the children to work in pairs and one of them is to dramatise being a good persuader to their partner. Change over. (Don't ever ask them to role play a bad persuader.) Encourage the children to show their role plays to the rest of the class.

Use this theme for an assembly; ask parents, visitors or another class to come and look at the children's work and present some of the drama.

When you're feeling sad and blue
and you dont know what to do
clap your hands and sing a song
that'll help the day along.

Theme 7 Citizenship

1. Why do we need rules?

2. Rules outside school

3. Who makes the rules?

4. Other people's property and feelings

5. Being truthful

6. Losing and finding

7. Litter

8. Protecting our environment.

This will help the environment.

Explain to the children exactly what a haiku is. They don't have to abide by the 5-7-5 rule when they compose their own.

| **A haiku is a:** |
| Poem in three lines |
| Five syllables, then seven |
| Five again. No rhyme. |

The following haiku can be used in this section:

Why do we need rules?	**Being truthful**
Rules can keep us safe	Telling lies is wrong.
They help us know what to do.	It never makes things better
Keep them when you can.	Best to tell the truth.
Rules outside school	**Losing and finding**
Stay on the pavement.	We hate to lose things,
Never run into the road.	It makes us feel unhappy.
Rules can keep us safe.	Finding things is good.
Who makes the rules?	**Litter**
We can make some rules	Don't ever drop bits
That help us to behave well.	Always put them in the bin.
Breaking rules is wrong.	Litter makes a mess.
Other people's property and feelings	**Protecting our environment**
We take care of things	We live in a world
We don't leave a mess about,	That is a beautiful place.
And don't hurt feelings.	Keep it looking good.

Citizenship – younger children

1. Why do we need rules?

Ask the children to think about how you organise the classroom and what rules you have.

Give them examples such as what do you do:

- with wet paintings, finished work
- at register time
- when play is over
- when people want to change activities
- about shouting, fighting
- in Circle Time.

10 children think the important rule for Circle Time is to listen carefully.

Stand and tell

Ask volunteers to think of a good rule for your classroom.

'A good rule for our classroom rule is ...'

Make a list of what they say and read out the rules they have told you.

Ask them to choose which they think is the most important rule from the list.

Stand, count and sit down quickly

Ask all children to stand. If they chose the first rule on the list, they raise a hand, and count themselves. As the children count themselves write the number against the rule; tell these children to sit down.

Go through your list until all the children are sitting. Make a display with this data if you wish, adding children's pictures or pictures from magazines.

Haiku

Read this haiku to the children. Talk about the importance of rules. Explain that rules are there to help us to know what to do and how to act in different circumstances.

> **Why do we need rules?**
> Rules can keep us safe.
> They help us know what to do.
> Keep them when you can.

Help children to make a class haiku about why rules are important in the wider community.

Further work

Ask the children to draw a picture of themselves keeping one of the rules and help them to add a caption to explain this. Display this work alongside your list of rules.

1. Why do we need rules?

Ask the children to think about what might happen if we didn't have any rules at all. Give some examples – such as:

- what could happen in the classroom if there weren't any rules
- what might happen on roads if we didn't keep to the left and obey signals
- what could happen in shops if we didn't queue?

Pass the sentence

'If we didn't have rules ...'

Share ideas

When all the children have had their turn ask them to think of the most important rules you have in school or in the classroom. Ask the children to go to their working groups to talk about classroom rules and to jot down what they think are the three most important rules in the classroom.

> We think the 3 important rules in our classroom are:
> 1. work quietly
> 2. wait your turn
> 3. listen to others.
>
> Ajit, Bob, Asher, Liam, Shola, Kerm.

Come back together and ask each group to stand up while one child tells their group's three most important rules.

Haiku

Read and talk about the haiku on the facing page. Ask the children to suggest words they could use for a haiku about rules and list these on the board. Ask them to work in pairs to compose, write and illustrate a haiku, using words from the list or their own words. Ask them to choose a good title for their haiku.

Further work

Ask the children to draw and write a slogan for one rule.

Children could vote on the one most important rule or put classroom rules in their order of importance.

Ask the children to look out for safety rules they might see when they are out and about – e.g. 'No cycling', 'Danger'. Ask them to write these down to discuss at the next Circle Time or when doing the next section, 'Rules outside school'. You could make a display of these.

2. Rules outside school

Pass the sentence

Remind the children about the rules you have in school and tell them one of your own home rules. Ask them to think of one rule they have in their home.

'One rule we have at home is ...'

Stand up if .../Change places

Say to the children 'If you know what would happen if you broke the rule you told us, stand up, then change places.'

Pass the sentence

Now ask the children to think of rules we have outside school.

'My outside school rule is ...'

> **Home rules**
>
> Wipe your shoes on the mat when you come indoors.

Stand up if .../Change places

Ask the children to stand up and change places if they know what might happen if they broke that rule. (You might like to explore this further if the children want to talk about it.)

Haiku

Read this haiku to the children. Talk about their role in keeping safety rules. Explain that these rules are made so that everyone will know what to do and so everyone will be safe. Ask them to think of a rule about how everyone can keep safe near roads – cyclists, walkers and vehicle drivers. Help them to make a class haiku about this.

> **Rules outside school**
>
> Stay on the pavement.
>
> Never run into the road.
>
> Rules can keep us safe.

Further work

Explore with the children the rules of various places and situations – e.g. the library, on a bus, in a restaurant, on a picnic, at the seaside, at the dentist, in someone's house, with a dog, with a bicycle, at the swimming pool. Write these on the board and add any others that the children suggest.

Ask each group to choose one of these situations and ask each child in the group to write and illustrate good rules for that place or situation. Display these rules and ask the children to suggest a heading for the display.

2. Rules outside school

Stand and tell

Ask the children to think of the rules in your city, town or village. Tell them that these are often called laws or by-laws. Can they think of any of these rules?

Ask volunteers to tell you the rules they know.

Pass the sentence

Can they think of a rule that children have to remember?

   'A rule or law that children have to remember is ...'

A rule is not to take things that don't belong to you.

Stand and tell

Ask volunteers to tell about any people whose job it is to help us keep these rules.

Stand and tell

Ask volunteers to stand and explain what they think might happen to grown-ups who break rules or laws.

Discuss what the children offer and correct any if necessary.

Policemen help us to keep some rules. They stop people from driving too fast.

Haiku

Read and talk about the haiku on the facing page. Ask the children to suggest words they could use for a haiku about rules in various places and list these on the board. Ask them to work in pairs to compose, write and illustrate a haiku, using words from the list or their own words. Ask them to choose a good title for their haiku.

Further work

Help the children to find out about local laws.

NO PARKING

- How do people know about them?
- Are there reminders (notices) to keep laws anywhere in your area?
- How do people try to make sure they are kept?
- What happens to people who don't keep them?

Ask the children to draw and write about rules in the wider community to make a display to share with others in school.

3. Who makes the rules?

Stand and tell

Ask the children to think about the rules they have been talking about in other Circle Times. Ask them to stand up if they can say who makes the rules for the school.

Make a list of what they say. Read your list with the children and ask if they know who is in charge of the whole school. Does that person make all the rules? Explain about higher authorities and that even important people, such as the head teacher, have to obey rules.

> **School rules**
> Our teachers make some rules.
> Our head teacher makes some rules.
> Governors make some rules.
> The local office people make some rules.
> The government make some rules.

Stand, tell and sit down quickly

Ask the children to say 'yes' or 'no' if they think having rules is a good idea.

Pass the sentence

Ask why we need rules at school.

   'I think we need rules because …'

Ask the children to think of what might happen if we did not have rules at school.

'I think if we didn't have rules …'

Rules are a good idea. They help us to know what to do.

Haiku

Read this haiku to the children. Talk about their role in making and keeping school rules. Choose one school rule and ask the children to help you write a haiku about it. Can you make other haiku about other rules?

> **Who makes the rules?**
> We can make some rules
> That help us to behave well.
> Breaking rules is wrong.

Ask the children to copy one of these to illustrate and choose some for a display.

Further work

Ask the children to think of some good rules for playing in the school playground. Ask them to decide (vote) on the most important playground rule. Print out and display this rule surrounded by pictures drawn by the children showing them obeying it.

3. Who makes the rules?

> People make local laws in the town hall. They are called councillors.

Stand and tell/Jot down

Ask the children to think of the by-laws and laws that we have. Invite them to stand and tell if they think they know who made them.

Jot down what the children say. Read your list.

Stand and tell

Ask the children to think of how people agree about which laws to make or change; ask volunteers to stand and tell how they think people decide.

Help the children to understand about voting and democratic decisions and that even when people don't agree they have to abide by the decision of the majority.

Compare this to how school decisions are made by teachers and governors.

Compare this to how you and the children make decisions about things in class.

Pass the sentence

Ask the children to think of what could happen if we did not have laws.

GO TO PRISON

'If we didn't have laws ...'

Ask the children to think about what should happen to people who break laws. Ask them to focus on one rule or law. What would they do to someone who broke it?

'If someone broke this rule or law, I think they should ...'

Haiku

Read and talk about the haiku on the facing page. Ask the children to suggest words they could use for a haiku about the various people who make rules in society. List these people on the board. Ask them to work in pairs to compose, write and illustrate a haiku about these people making rules or laws. Ask them to illustrate and choose a good title for their haiku.

Further work

Ask the children to find out about local councillors. Ask them to write about the job of councillor and make a display of this work.

Arrange a visit to the local magistrate's or county court or ask a local magistrate to come to school to talk to the children about their work. Talk about the jury system.

4. Other people's property and feelings

Remind the children that they have to take care of things that belong to other people as well as things that belong to them. Ask if they can remember having something that belonged to someone else and how they took care of it.

Tell a story

> Ranjit had borrowed a book from the library and he read it in his room. He went downstairs, with the book, for a drink of cola and his Mum told him to drink it downstairs and not to spill it. He was reading when his baby sister toddled over to him. She pulled his arm and the drink spilt – all over the book.

Pass the sentence

How do you think Ranjit, his mum, the librarian and the baby sister felt?

'I think ... felt ...'

Stand and tell

Can anyone tell what Ranjit should do?

List what the children say or discuss this. Read your list and ask the children to tell you what they think is the best thing Ranjit could do.

> We think Ranjit should:
>
> dry the book
> tell the librarian and say 'sorry'
> say he would buy another book
> make sure he was more careful next time.

Haiku

Read this haiku to the children. Talk about their role in taking care of other people's things. Ask the children to help you write a haiku about it.

> **Other people's property and feelings**
> We take care of things.
> We don't leave a mess about,
> And don't hurt feelings.

Ask the children to copy and illustrate this haiku. Choose one to display.

Further work

Talk about other similar disasters and discuss what could be done to repair the situation. Tell the children that saying and being 'sorry' are important but ask them how they can make sure it doesn't happen again.

Ask them to draw a picture of some occasion when they did something to spoil someone's property and to write in a speech bubble what they said to that person.

4. Other people's property and feelings

Pass the sentence

Ask the children how they feel when they break or spoil things or when they see broken things. Choose one of these or use both for half the children.

'When I see broken things I feel ...'
'When I break or spoil things I feel ...'

Explore some of the words the children used. Did some of the words mean the same? Did some mean the opposite? Did some children use the same words to complete both the sentences?

Stand and tell

Ask the children to think of a time when they had to take great care of something very special. Tell us about what happened.

Pass the sentence

Remind the children that even when things are not especially precious they should take care not to break or spoil them. Ask the children to think of something they always have to take great care of.

'I always take care of ...'

When I hurt Sara's feelings she cried. I said I was sorry.

Haiku

Read and talk about the haiku on the facing page. Talk about their role in taking care of other people's feelings. Ask the children to think of a time when their feelings were hurt. How did they feel? What did they do? Ask the children to compose and illustrate a haiku about not hurting people's feelings. Choose some to display.

Further work

Remind the children that other people's feelings are important and that they have to take care not to hurt them. Ask if they can remember when they hurt someone's feelings. How did they feel? How did the person feel? What did they, themselves, do or say to try to make things better? Make a display of children's drawings and writing on this theme for parents and other children.

5. Being truthful

Ask the children if they have ever found it difficult to tell the truth because they were afraid of getting into trouble. Tell them that we all make mistakes and that it is only fair to own up to them and to say we are sorry. (If you can, tell of some experience of yours when it was difficult for you to own up.)

Pass the face

Ask the children to think of how their face would look if they were not telling the truth and pass their face around the circle.

Tell them that a good way to tell the truth is to start by saying 'Yes, I'm sorry I …'

Talk about people telling a lie because they are afraid of getting found out about something they did wrong. Explain that it might seem to be a good way out but that people often get found out and then find it has made things worse.

> **How I showed I was sorry:**
>
> I said I'd not do it again
> I tried to mend it
> I said I didn't mean it
> I gave my Mum a kiss
> I cleared up the mess
> I'll try to be more careful
> I'll think before I do things
> I'll watch what I'm doing.

Stand and tell

Can any volunteer tell of some time when they told a lie and why they did it?

'I told a lie when …'

Explain that it is better to tell the truth and say they are sorry. Reassure them that it is often hard for people to say sorry, even when they feel sorry inside.

Next ask them to think of a way that people can show they are sorry.

Haiku

Read this haiku to the children. Help them to learn it. Ask the children to help you to write a class haiku about being truthful. Ask them to copy and illustrate it.

> **Being truthful**
> Telling lies is wrong.
> It never makes things better.
> Best to tell the truth.

Further work

Ask the children to think of some time when it was hard to tell the truth. Talk about 'owning up'. Explain that people won't believe anything you say if they know you tell lies. Ask them to draw a picture of themselves telling the truth.

5. Being truthful

Pass the face

Ask the children to think of a time when they found it hard to 'own up' to doing something wrong or to a mistake they made. Ask them to show how they felt, then pass the face around the circle.

Stand and tell

Can the children think of a word to describe how they felt? Collect the words they suggest and read them back to them.

Repeat the above, this time asking the children to tell how they felt when they had owned up and told the truth.

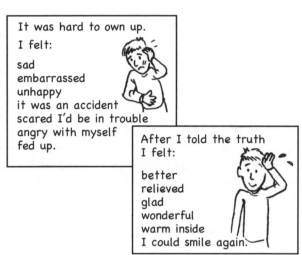

It was hard to own up.
I felt:
sad
embarrassed
unhappy
it was an accident
scared I'd be in trouble
angry with myself
fed up.

After I told the truth
I felt:
better
relieved
glad
wonderful
warm inside
I could smile again.

Pass the sentence

Talk about the difference between acting or pretending and real life. Ask the children to tell about what they like to pretend to do or be.

'I like to pretend ... but it's not the truth.'

Haiku

Read and talk about the haiku on the facing page. Talk about the importance of being truthful so that other people will know that what they say is always the truth. Ask the children to compose and illustrate a haiku about being truthful. Choose some to display.

Further work

Make two charts to display the words the children gave you about how they felt:

- when they found it hard to own up
- after they had owned up.

Ask the children to work in pairs to write about why it is important to tell the truth. Display some of this work around your two charts.

Read or tell the story about the boy who cried 'wolf'.

6. Losing and finding

Talk to the children about how we feel if we lose something.

Stand and tell

Ask volunteers to stand and tell you what they lost and how they felt. Collect the 'feelings' words.

Pass the sentence

Now ask them how they felt when they found it (or something else they had lost) again and collect these words.

'When I found it I felt ...'

I felt very sad when I lost my teddy. I cried.

Stand and tell

Ask volunteers to stand and tell you if they have ever found anything that belonged to someone else; to say what they found and what they did. Remind them how the person might have felt if they lost something they treasured.

When I found my toy car I felt so glad and happy again.

Pass the sentence

'If you find something, you should ...'
'If you find something, you shouldn't ...'

Haiku

Read this haiku to the children. Talk about what they do in your school if they find something. Look at the two lists of 'feelings' words and ask the children to help you to compose two haiku – one about how you feel when you lose something, the other about your feelings when you find something you've lost.

Losing and finding
We hate to lose things,
It makes us feel unhappy.
Finding things is good.

Further work

Ask the children to draw a picture of themselves either with something they have lost or something they lost and have found again.

Ask the children to tell you about their feelings when they lost or found this object (or person). Display their pictures in the two groups with the words they told you in large speech bubbles alongside the two illustrated class haiku.

Read stories to the children on this theme – such as *Dogger* by Shirley Hughes (Red Fox, 1993).

6. Losing and finding

Pass the sentence

Ask the children to think about how they feel when they lose something.

'When I lose something I feel ...'

Now ask the children to think of some of the things they might find when they are out and about. Remind them that these could be valuable, interesting, dirty or dangerous.

Pass the sentence

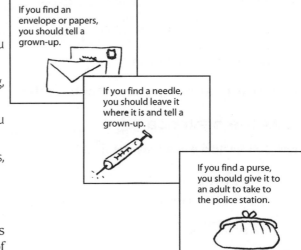

If you find an envelope or papers, you should tell a grown-up.

If you find a needle, you should leave it where it is and tell a grown-up.

If you find a purse, you should give it to an adult to take to the police station.

'If you find something valuable, you should ...'

'If you find something interesting, you should ...'

'If you find something dirty, you should ...'

'If you find something dangerous, you should ...'

Share ideas

Split the children into four groups and ask each group to take one of the above and make a list of items they might find under those headings. Ask them to write what they should do with each item and why.

Come together in a group or circle and ask a spokesperson from each group to tell you about their lists.

Haiku

Read and talk about the haiku on the facing page. Talk about the importance of being honest and doing the correct thing when you find objects. Ask the children to compose and illustrate a haiku about losing something precious. Choose some to display.

Further work

Talk to the children of the dangers touching dangerous objects such as needles, syringes or spent cartridges. Make sure they know what to do if they find these items.

Ask each group to look at their list of items, decide what to do with each thing and make an illustrated chart, showing each item and what to do if they find it. Display the four charts where everyone in the school can see them.

7. Litter

Ask the children to think about what to do with things they no longer want to keep – such as ice-cream papers or sweet wrappers.

Stand up, count and sit down quickly (three times)

Ask children to stand and say 'yes' or 'no' if they think they should:

We think litter is:

horrid
awful
disgusting
messy
smelly
horrible
spoils things
makes things look bad.

Don't drop it – ever.

- throw litter down in the street
- put it in a litter bin
- take it home with them.

What happens to these papers if they do each one?

Pass the sentence

How do they feel when they see litter?

'When I see litter I feel ...'
'When I see litter I think ...'

Stand and tell

Ask volunteers to say what they think happens to things that are thrown away.

Haiku

Read this haiku to the children. Help them to learn it. Ask the children to help you write a class haiku about not dropping litter. Ask them to copy and illustrate it. Choose some to display.

> **Litter**
> Don't ever drop bits
> Always put them in the bin.
> Litter makes a mess.

Further work

Talk to the children about things that can be recycled – such as paper and cans. Ask volunteers to tell you about the recycling scheme in your area and the kinds of things that are recycled.

Talk about what happens to things that cannot be recycled. Do they know that they are dumped in a great hole and covered over? Ask the children to tell you if they can think of anything old that their family uses again (recycles) for a different purpose – e.g. does Dad use old shirts as cleaning cloths for the car?

7. Litter

Pass the sentence

Talk to children about litter and the way some people drop it just anywhere. What would they say to people who drop litter?

'I would say ...'

Pass the sentence

Now talk to them about the difficulties of disposing of unwanted goods.

Ask them to think of what people can do with things they no longer want.

'If you don't want it any more, you could ...'

> Get rid of things you don't want this way:
>
> sell them
> take them to charity shops
> recycle them yourself
> put them in the dustbin
> take them to the dump
> put them in recycle sacks
> take them to the garden waste dump
> take them to recycling bins.

Remind the children that we sometimes use junk materials to make things in the classroom.

Share ideas

Ask them to work in pairs or threes and make a list of all the different bits of junk they have used to make things. After three minutes ask one child from each group to stand up and read out their list.

Haiku

Read and talk about the haiku on the facing page. Talk about the importance of not dropping litter and that it could be dangerous to pick up someone else's litter. Explain that it could be dangerous to put their hand inside a litter bin because there might be something sharp inside.

Ask the children to compose and illustrate a haiku about doing the right thing with litter. Choose some to display.

Further work

This could include finding out about the local rubbish disposal.

- Are there tips or dumps for large item such as beds?
- What happens to old cars?
- Does their local authority have a garden waste recycling programme?
- Who wants old clothes?
- What happens to school rubbish?

8. Protecting our environment

Ask the children if they know what the word 'environment' means.

Stand and tell

Ask volunteers to stand and tell you what the word 'environment' means to them. Make a list of what they say. If no one knows, explain that it means the surroundings – the area around where we live, the natural world and the countryside.

Pass the sentence

Ask the children to think of all the beautiful things in our environment.

'Our environment is beautiful because ...'

Discuss what the children say.

Who looks after the environment?

farmers
country people
street sweepers
park-keepers
painters
people who mend things
people who put flowers out.

Stand and tell

Ask the children to stand up if they can think of someone who is responsible for keeping the environment looking good.

We can:

keep it tidy
take care of things
enjoy the flowers
not spoil things
help the caretaker.

Pass the sentence

Ask the children what they themselves can do.

'We can ...'

Protect our environment
We live in a world
That is a beautiful place.
Keep it looking good.

Haiku

Read this haiku to the children. Look at the list of words you made about the environment and ask the children to use some of these words to help you to compose one or more haiku.

Further work

Ask the children to look around the school and grounds for things that have been put there to make it more beautiful. Can they make a list of them?

Ask them to suggest other things that your school could do to make the school environment outside better – such as planting trees or springtime bulbs, planting tubs of flowers, making a quiet area for playtimes or creating shade for sunny days.

8. Protecting our environment

Pass the sentence

Ask the children to think of one thing they can do to keep their school environment looking good.

'To keep our school environment looking good we could ...'

List what the children say, noting the number of repeats.

Stand and tell

Ask the children if they know who makes, mends or puts beautiful and interesting things in our environment – e.g. street furniture such as seats, plants, notices. Collect the children's responses and use these to make a list of 'environment improvers'.

Stand, tell and sit down quickly

Remind the children that some people spoil the environment by leaving litter, breaking things or spraying with spray paints. Ask them to say 'yes' or 'no' to show whether they think they will spoil things when they are bigger.

Environment improvers

Shopkeepers put flowers outside.
The council people put out seats and litter boxes.
Dustbin men take our rubbish away.
Street sweepers clean the roads and pavements.
People mend the lights.
People paint the lamp-posts.
People plant trees and flowers.

Pass the sentence

Ask what they think of people who spoil the environment.

'I think ...'

Haiku

Read and talk about the haiku on the facing page. Talk about the importance of protecting our local environment. Ask the children to compose and illustrate a haiku about doing that. Choose some to display.

Further work

Ask the children to look around your locality for things that have been put there to make it more attractive. You could take the children on a 'looking walk' around the school grounds or locality. Make a list of all the things that make your environment more beautiful. Talk about preserving things in the wider world – such as rain forests, animals or plants that are likely to become extinct.

Let's celebrate citizenship!

In Circle Time talk with the children about all the work they have done about citizenship. Praise their illustrations and writing. Praise them for their work and for their learning.

Pass the sentence

Ask the children to tell you what they have learned about rules.

'I know that …'

Ask them to tell you what they have learned about being truthful.

'I know that …'

Ask them to tell you what they have learned about other people's things, feelings and litter.

'I know that …'

Ask them to tell you some of the things they can do to protect the environment.

'I could …'

Extension activities

Use a drama session to ask the children in pairs to role play someone who is saying sorry for telling a lie and someone who is going to forgive them. What will they say? What will they do?

Ask older children to draw a picture of an endangered animal or plant and to write what we could do to keep it from extinction.

Ask the children to compose the words to a song about our beautiful, wonderful world. Ask them to try to fit the words to a well-known song or nursery rhyme tune.

Use this theme for an assembly; ask parents, visitors or another class to come and look at the children's work and present some of the drama.

> To the tune of three blind mice
>
> We have a wonderful world.
> Let's keep it safe.
> We all must keep it safe.
> Try to keep the environment swell.
> Tidy and clean and protect it as well.

Theme 8 Loss, grief and separation

1. Losing something
2. Feeling sad
3. Missing someone
4. Someone's leaving
5. Changes
6. Poor Grandma.

I feel really sad about it.

Explain to the children exactly what a haiku is. They don't have to abide by the 5-7-5 rule when they compose their own.

A haiku is a:
Poem in three lines
Five syllables, then seven
Five again. No rhyme.

The following haiku can be used in this section:

Losing something When you lose a toy It makes you feel bad inside. Let's hope you find it.	**Someone's leaving** When my sister leaves We can phone her and text her. One day she'll return.
Feeling sad Many kinds of things Can make you feel sad and hurt. You try to cheer up.	**Changes** When Mum and Dad split I thought it was all my fault They wanted to go.
Missing someone My friend is going To a place far, far away. How can I bear it?	**Poor Grandma** Grandma's very ill. She stays in bed all the day. I'm sad she might die.

1. Losing something

When I lost my dinner money I felt ...

Pass the sentence

Ask the children if they have ever lost something and invite a few volunteers to raise a hand and tell you.

'I once lost ...'

Jot down

Make a list on the board and then read it to the children. Can you group these things into some kind of order – such as toys, games, books, money? Ask them to think about the worst kinds of things to lose and draw a ring around these.

Pass the sentence

Ask them to think about their feelings when they had lost the most important things from the list.

'When I lost . . . I felt ...'

Make a list of these feelings and ask the children to think why they felt like this. Was it because what they lost was special, valuable, old, much loved?

'I felt ... because ...'

Haiku

Read this haiku to the children. Look at the list of words you made about the things the children had lost and how they felt and ask the children to use some of the 'feelings' words to help you to compose one or more haiku.

> **Losing something**
> When you lose a toy
> It makes you feel bad inside.
> Let's hope you find it.

Further work

Ask the children to reflect on these sad feelings and to say whether they cried about losing this thing. Explain that it is OK to be sad when you lose something but that crying won't bring the thing back.

Talk about what they could have done to try to find it and collect sentences from the children. Write these up in speech bubbles and display them near some of the haiku.

1. Losing something

Losing something
I felt ...
cross
angry with myself
I was careless
it wasn't my fault
it just wasn't fair
someone moved it
it can't have gone
who's got it?

Touch your ...

Talk to the children about a time when you lost something special and how you felt.

Ask the children to touch their nose if they have ever lost something really special. Ask volunteers to say what they lost and how they felt.

Next ask them to touch their ear if they have ever had different feelings about losing something and make a list of these. Perhaps they felt cross with themselves or thought someone had taken it.

Pass the sentence

Ask the children to think about what they said or did when they lost this thing.

'When I lost ... I ...'

Make a list of these feelings. Ask the children if any of them can remember finding something that they had lost. How did they feel?

'When I found ... I felt ...'

Make a list of these feelings. Are they the opposite of the feelings on the first list? Would some of them make opposite pairs?

Haiku

Read and talk about the haiku on the facing page. Ask the children to work in pairs and use some of the 'feelings' words to compose two haiku – one about losing and one about finding something precious or special. Can they write these out as a pair and illustrate them? Choose some to display.

Further work

Ask the children to finish writing this story and to say how Tom felt at the beginning, in the middle, and at the end of the story.

Tom had 50p pocket money and he wanted to buy some gel pens so that he could do some drawing and colouring. When he got to the shop he felt in his pocket and there was no money there. He felt ...

Ask some of the children to read out their stories in Circle Time. Ask them to vote on the ones to display or put into a class storybook.

2. Feeling sad

Pass the sentence

Talk to the children about sad feelings and explain that it is OK to feel like this when they are sad about something. Talk about the kinds of things that make them feel sad.

'I'd feel sad if ...'

Make a list of the things that make children sad.

```
I'd feel sad if ...
I was ill
my mum wasn't there
I did something bad
I lost something
my sister wasn't here
I broke something
I was in trouble
I couldn't do my work
someone was cross with me
```

Share ideas

Talk about each one on the list and how you could make yourself feel a bit better. Discuss the kinds of things that children can do to make themselves feel better.

Pass the sentence/Change places

Talk about whereabouts in their body they feel these sad feelings – in their head, heart, tummy, dry mouth.

'I feel sadness in my ...'

Ask children who repeat words to change places.

Stand and tell

Remind the children that they can help other children who feel sad to feel better. Ask volunteers to suggest what they could say to someone who felt sad, in various situations – such as if they were ill, if their mum was in hospital, if they had lost something or if they had to wait their turn for the computer. Make a list of good things to say.

Talk about and display this list.

Haiku

Read this haiku to the children. Look at the list of words you made about feeling sad and ask the children to use some of these words to help you to compose one or more haiku.

> **Feeling sad**
> Many kinds of things
> Can make you feel sad and hurt.
> You try to cheer up.

Further work

Ask the children to help you to make two lists – one of what they can do to help themselves to feel better when they are sad and the other a list of things they can do or say to cheer up people who feel sad.

2. Feeling sad

Pass the sentence

Explain that it is normal and healthy to feel sad sometimes. Some things that make us sad are trivial and other things are more important. Ask the children to tell you some of the not really important things that make them feel sad.

'It makes me feel sad when ...'

Stand and tell

Ask volunteers to tell of really serious things that can make us sad. Discuss each of these.

Tell a story

Rashid used to live in Pakistan. His father is a doctor. One day his father said that they were all going to move to England because he had got a new job here in a hospital. They had to leave lots of things behind – their house, family, friends and pets. Rashid was sad about leaving his home and leaving lots of toys behind. He also felt worried about moving to a new country.

Pass the sentence

Ask the children to think about Rashid's feelings.

'I think Rashid would feel ...'

If they were Rashid, what things would they miss most?

'I would miss ... most.'

Ask the children how this would make them feel. Collect their 'feelings' words.

I think Rashid would feel ...
sad
worried
unhappy
scared
fed up
miserable
apprehensive
frightened
fearful.

Haiku

Read and talk about the haiku on the facing page. Ask each child to compose and illustrate a haiku about being sad, using some of the 'feelings' words. Choose some to display.

Further work

Ask the children to talk to their families at home about their sad feelings and to ask them what they do when they feel sad. Ask them to make a list in two columns – one naming the sadness and alongside what the person does to help them. Ask them to bring this to the next Circle Time to share with everyone.

3. Missing someone

Stand and tell

Ask the children if they have ever been lost. Ask volunteers to say how they felt about this.

When I got lost, I felt ...
worried
sad
unhappy
frightened
scared.

Ask all the children to think about how a child would feel if they were lost and how an adult would feel if they could not find them. Would these be the same feelings?

Pass the sentence

Ask the children to close their eyes and think of all the people in their network of family and friends. Ask them to think of just one of these people and to open their eyes.

'My person is ...'

Now ask them what they would miss most if this person were to go away for a short time.

'If they went away, I would miss ...'

What kinds of things could they do to stay in touch?

'I could ...'

Haiku

Read this haiku to the children. Look at the list of words you made about how you felt when you were lost. Ask them to use some of these words to help you compose one or more haiku about missing someone who goes away for a short time.

> **Missing someone**
> My friend is going
> To a place far, far away.
> How can I bear it?

Further work

Ask the children to think of a time when they missed someone; perhaps missing a parent when a babysitter was looking after them or when having a sleepover at a friend's. Ask them to draw themselves missing the absent person and help them to write who the person was and why they were not there. Can they draw the missing person in a bubble?

Loss, grief and separation – older children

3. Missing someone

Remind the children of the story of Rashid and how he came to England, leaving so many things and people behind. Talk about how Rashid would feel when he left all his friends and relatives behind. Ask the children to think about how they would feel if they left all their friends and relatives behind and moved to a new country where lots of things were different.

I think it would be better to stay behind with everyone I know here.

Pass the sentence

'If I moved away, I would feel ...'

Touch your ...

Ask the children to think about whether it would be better to be the one to go or the one to stay behind.

Ask those who think it would be better to be the one to go away to touch their nose and ask volunteers to say why.

Ask the other children to volunteer to say why they think it would be better to stay behind.

Stand and show

Ask the children to work in pairs and to think about one person leaving and the other staying behind. Ask them to write down what each person would say. Ask volunteer pairs to role play this to the circle.

Haiku

Read and talk about the haiku on the facing page. Ask each child to compose and illustrate a haiku about missing someone they know who is going away for a short time. Choose some to display.

Further work

Ask the children to think of the time when they moved to their present class and left their old teacher or pre-school teacher behind. Ask them to draw a picture of that person and to write about some of the things they remember doing when they were in that class or pre-school. Do they still see this person? How does that make them feel?

4. Someone's leaving

Talk with the children about people growing up and leaving home. Tell them how your family felt when you left home, perhaps to go to college or to live somewhere else. Tell them how you felt to be moving on. Talk about how the people left behind might have felt.

They would feel …
unhappy
not wanted
left behind
left out
not important.

Pass the sentence

'I think people left behind would feel …'

Tell a story

Mark was 18 years old and he left home for a year to go to work abroad as a helper in a school in Africa. He wanted to help people who went to school where there were few teachers, hardly any books, where there were no computers or whiteboards. Mark's younger brother Jon felt very sad when his brother went. He cried a lot and was really grumpy. Jon's parents reminded him that Mark would come back after a year but that didn't stop Jon feeling bad.

Hands-up session

Ask the children to raise a hand if they can suggest what Jon and his family can do so that they don't miss Mark too much. Make a list of their suggestions on separate pieces of paper. When everyone has had a turn, put three hoops into the middle of the circle. Label each one 'Really good idea', 'Quite good idea', 'Not such a good idea'. Ask the children to help you to put the slips of paper into the most appropriate hoop.

Haiku

Read this haiku to the children. Look at the list of words you have in the 'Really good idea' hoop and ask the children to use some of these words to help you to compose one or more haiku.

> **Someone's leaving**
> When my sister leaves
> We can phone her and text her.
> One day she'll return.

Further work

Ask the children to draw two pictures – one of someone leaving their family and the other of the same person keeping in touch with the family left behind. Help them to write a sentence about each picture.

4. Someone's leaving

Read the story on the facing page about Mark going to another country for a year. Ask the children if any of their family has done something like this. Can they tell the class about it?

Imagine it

Ask the children to close their eyes and try to imagine how it would be if it were their brother, sister or friend who was going away for a year. Ask them to open their eyes and invite volunteers to tell the group how they would feel. Make a list of these feelings on the board. Explain that these feelings are quite natural and that the person leaving would know about how they would feel.

Keeping in touch
letters
postcards
phone calls
emails
faxes
visits
computer link-ups
presents.

Ask the children to think about how the person leaving would feel and to suggest 'feelings' words to make a second list. Are any of the words in the two lists the same? Are any opposites?

Remind the children that as we grow and grow up there will be many reasons for such separations and that it's hard to let people go but you have to smile, let them go and just make every effort to keep in touch. Ask the children to think of all the ways we can keep in touch with people who move away.

Haiku

Read and talk about the haiku on the facing page. Ask each child to read through the two lists of 'feelings' words and use some to compose and illustrate a haiku about someone who is leaving. Read them in Circle Time and vote on one to display.

Further work

Talk with the children about parents who have to work away from home. Perhaps some are in the forces and are away for a long time. Others may have jobs that take them away from home during the week.

Ask them to write a story about a grown-up who had to live away from home at times and how their family felt every time they had to say goodbye.

5. Changes

Talk to the children about the changes in their short lifetimes. First they were babies and then toddlers; now they are at school. Ask them to think of any changes in their family circumstances – such as a new baby or moving house.

My family changed ...
Josef was born
Dad got a new job
we moved to this flat
my brother went to college
Grandad died
Auntie came to live here
we got a puppy.

Pass the sentence/Change places

'My family changed when ...'

Children who come up with the same phrases should change places.

Make a list of these changes on the board and talk about them and any others you can think of.

Share ideas

Explain that things are always changing in families and that as they grow and grow up there will be more changes. Talk about good changes when something pleasant happens and bad changes when something sad happens; temporary changes and permanent changes.

Stand and tell

- Ask volunteers to tell about happy changes in their family.
- Ask volunteers to tell about temporary changes in their family.
- Ask volunteers to tell about permanent changes in their family.

Share ideas

Talk to the children about sad changes in their family – such as when people leave. Explain that these changes happen because the older people themselves want to make changes and that it is never because of the children.

Haiku

Read this haiku to the children. Look at the kinds of changes you discussed and ask the children to use the ideas to help you to compose a haiku.

> **Changes**
> When Mum and Dad split
> I thought it was all my fault
> They wanted to go.

Further work

Ask the children to draw a picture of a happy change in their family and to illustrate this. Share this work in Circle Time. If you can, read *Once There Were Giants* by Martin Waddell (Walker, 1991).

5. Changes

Talk to the children about the changes in their families. Explain that grown-ups sometimes want to make changes that children don't like and that there are many reasons for this. Sometimes the children don't like the changes but it is never their fault.

Tell a story

> When Tariq was six years old his parents decided to separate and go to live in different houses. Tariq and his older sister Amera were allowed to choose which house they went to live in. Tariq was upset and cried for a long time.
> He wanted to live with both his parents.

Stand and tell

Ask the children to think of what they could say to Tariq to help him to feel better about this change. Give the opportunity for all the children to have their say. Make notes of their suggestions.

What would you say?

Stay with your Mum
Stay with your Dad
You can visit them both
They'll take you on holidays
You'll have two homes.
It's not your fault.
They will both still love you.

Imagine it/Jot down

Ask the children to close their eyes and think of how all these four people would feel about the change. Ask them to work in pairs and jot down words to describe these kinds of feelings. Do they think all the people will feel the same? Will the children have the same feelings as the parents?

Ask them to list these feelings on small pieces of paper, share them with another pair and make a new list. Share this new list with another four and make a new one to bring to the circle. Read out the feelings and make one final list.

Haiku

Read and talk about the haiku on the facing page. Ask groups of children to use the final list of feelings and use these ideas to make haiku from the point of view of the different people in Tariq's family. Share these in Circle Time.

Further work

Ask the children to draw four pictures of the four people in the story and write about how each is feeling about the changes in their family life.

6. Poor Grandma

Talk to the children about any pets they have. Do they know that pets do not normally live as long as people?

My old person is the man next door. We look after his dog when he goes on holiday.

Stand and tell

Ask volunteers to talk about any pets they have had that died and how they felt when this happened. Did they cry? How did other people in the family feel?

Read the story *I'll Always Love You* by Hans Wilheim (Hodder & Stoughton, 1985) and talk about how the different people in the story felt when the dog died. Remind them that babies are born, grow up into adults and one day, when they are old, they too will die. Explain that this is the normal life of a human person but that sometimes people have accidents or become ill and don't live quite so long. Remind them of the story *Once There Were Giants* (page 144).

Pass the sentence

Ask the children to think about an old person they know and talk about any funny, happy or interesting things they know about this person.

'My old person is ... and ....'

Allow children to pass but give them another opportunity at the end.

Ask the children to draw this old person and what they have told about them. Share these pictures in Circle Time before making them into a book of memories.

Haiku

Read this haiku to the children. Talk about how Grandma's children and grandchildren might feel about her being ill and staying in bed. Compose a class haiku about these feelings.

> **Poor Grandma**
> Grandma's very ill.
> She stays in bed all the day.
> I'm sad she might die.

Further work

Read stories of someone who dies or has memories to share – such as *Wilfred Gordon McDonald Partridge* by Mem Fox (Puffin Books, 1987) or *Granpa* by John Burningham (Puffin Books, 1988). Talk about the feelings of the people in each story. Ask children to illustrate part of one of the stories.

6. Poor Grandma

This person has wrinkles and his hair is white. I think he is quite old.

Talk to the children about how peoples' faces and bodies change as they grow and grow up.

Stand and tell

Ask them to cut out and bring in pictures of people's faces from old magazines at home. Put four hoops in the middle of the circle, each with a label – such as 'Very old', 'Quite old', 'Mums and Dads', 'Young'. Put all the pictures in a pile and ask each child in turn to take the top picture, show it to the group and explain why they are putting it into which hoop.

Now hold up of one of the pictures of an old person and ask volunteers to say how they know that the person is old.

Pass the sentence

Ask volunteers to tell the group something about themselves that they would want people to remember if they were not there any more.

'I would want them to remember ...'

Ask volunteers to tell the group about some interesting things about an old person they know. Talk about these interesting things as memories we would want to remember about this person if they died.

'I would want to remember ...'

Haiku

Read the haiku on the facing page to the children. Talk about how they would feel if it were their grandma. Ask them each to compare a haiku about an old person they know.

Further work

Read stories of someone who dies or has memories to share, such those as suggested on the facing page. Talk about the feelings of the people in each story. Ask children to illustrate part of one of the stories.

Let's celebrate loss, grief and separation

In Circle Time talk with the children about all the work they have done about loss, grief and separation. Praise their illustrations and writing. Praise them for their work and for their learning.

> **When I'm feeling sad**
> I try to cheer myself up –
> I make myself smile.

Pass this sentence

Ask the children to tell you what they have learned about losing something.

'I know that ...'

Ask them to tell you what they have learned about being sad.

'I know that ...'

Ask them to tell you what they have learned about changes in family life.

'I know that ...'

> **A feel better rap**
> It's OK to feel sad
> feel sad, feel sad.
> Everyone feels sad
> some times, some times.
> How can we feel better?
> Sing a song,
> Read a book
> Play football
> Hang out with friends.
> It's OK to feel sad
> BUT
> It's better to feel happy!

Extention activities

Ask the children to compose the words to a rap about being sad and what people can do to make themselves feel better.

Use a drama session to ask the children to depict the body language of people of various ages – babies, toddlers, parents, old people.

Ask older children to draw a series of four or six pictures of a boy or girl growing up to be old and to add a caption or writing about how these people have changed.

Resources

Picture storybooks

All these stories have a great deal to offer children as good stories in themselves and you can use them as a way in for discussion about all the themes covered in this book.

Friends and friendship

Fox, M. (1984) *Wilfred Gordon McDonald Partridge*, Puffin Books, London
Miss Nancy has lost her memory and Wilfred Gordon McDonald Partridge tries to help her find it. A book about memories.

Stimson, J. (1997) *A New Home for Tiger*, Scholastic, London
Tiger is excited because he and his mum are moving to a new house – but the enthusiasm soon fades when they reach their new home.

Wood, A. (1995) *Orlando's Little-While Friends*, Child's Play, Swindon
A young boy learns to overcome shyness and make friends. His feelings are recorded in this, his own illustrated scrapbook.

Growing and growing up

Anholt, C. and Anholt, L. (1991) *Aren't You Lucky!* Red Fox, London
A little girl is told that her mother is expecting another baby. The story follows the pregnancy up to the birth, the visit to hospital, the homecoming, and the difficulties and joys for the big sister of having a new baby in the house.

Hoffman, M. (1993) *Henry's Baby*, Dorling Kindersley, London
Who wants a baby in their house? Henry doesn't – at first. His friends, however, are delighted.

Sage, A. and Sage, C. (1991) *The Trouble with Babies*, Puffin Books, London
A child describes everything that is wrong with having a new baby in the house – the crying, dribbling and screaming – but then discovers that babies aren't that bad after all.

Talbot, J. (1989) *Hasn't He Grown?* Andersen Press, London
A picture book about growing up!

Feelings and persuasion

Blundell, T. (1993) *Oliver and the Monsters*, Viking Children's Books, London
Oliver's having trouble getting to sleep. He's not afraid of ghosts or the dark or anything but is plagued by an unruly bunch of monsters under his bed. They play in his bedroom, keep him awake and mess up his things. Then one night he decides that enough is enough and sets off through the deep, dark forest to the house where the monsters live.

Gliori, D. (1993) *A Lion at Bedtime*, Scholastic, London
Ben is frightened by a lion who visits him each night, until one snowy night Ben feels sorry for the poor animal. This delightful picture book is designed to be read to young children at bedtime, especially those who are scared at night time.

Hendry, D. (1996) *Dog Dottington*, Walker Books, London
The Dottington family is scared of something, so they decide to get a dog. They return from the Dogs' Home with a large, grey dog called Hero – but he's a true Dottington Dog, because he's scared of everything too! But in comforting Hero, the others forget their own fears.

Thomas, I. (1987) *Janine and the Carnival*, Scholastic, London
A carnival celebration in London is the setting for this story of a child who gets lost and is found again.

Citizenship

Hughes, S. (1993) *Dogger*, Red Fox, London
An award-winning story of how a beloved soft, brown toy called Dogger was lost and found. This book is a timeless classic which shows the distress the loss of a toy causes a child, as well as the reality of family life.

McKee, D. (2000) *Elmer and the Stranger,* Red Fox, London
A stranger called Kangaroo comes to the village; he likes jumping but keeps falling over. Elmer helps him to win the jumping competition and turns a stranger into a friend.

Vyner, T. (2002) *World Team*, Random House, London
All around the world millions of children are enjoying football. This book also looks at geography and the concept of time zones.

Moses, B. (1998) *It wasn't Me, Excuse Me, I'll Do It*, Weyland
These three books with funny, cartoon-style illustrations about honesty, politeness and responsibility will help children to understand citizenship values.

Keeping healthy

Oram, H.(2002) *Princess Camomile Gets her Way*, Andersen Press
Princess Camomile is not allowed ever so many things. Nanny Nettle is too strict – why, she even forbids her sweets at her own birthday party! So she slips out of the castle, and heads for Bagseye the bad cat's sweet shop – and a most unexpected adventure follows! As she tells Nanny, it's not sweets that make her sick – it's too many sweets!

Moore, I. (1996) *Six Dinner Sid*, McDonald Young Books
Sid, a devious but loveable cat, has six homes and so eats six dinners every day. This is great until he becomes ill and is taken to the vet (six times). Could he have to take six doses of medicine?

Cole, B. (2004) *Mummy Never Told Me*, Red Fox, London
What are tummy buttons for, and how do they get there? What does the tooth fairy really look like? Why do grown-ups have hair in their ears and up their noses, but

sometimes none on their heads? Why do Mummy and Daddy lock you out of their bedroom, and where do they go at night? Babette Cole explores these questions and many more with her wonderfully sharp text and riotously funny illustrations.

Puttock, S. (2001) *Squeaky Clean*, Red Fox, London
Three grubby little piglets do not want to be clean and won't be washed but Mama Pig knows how to turn bath time into fun.

Grey, K. (2001) *Who's Poorly Too?* Red Fox, London
Everyone is feeling poorly; the Dalmatian has come out in stripes and the centipede has sprained 96 ankles. However all's well that ends well and with a little help they're soon feeling better.

Rosen, M. (1999) *Lunch Boxes Don't Fly*, Puffin, London
Rosen's collection on the theme of food contains old and new material with rhythm and repetition.

London, J. (2001) *Froggy Goes to Bed*, Red Fox, London
Mum gets more and more sleepy as Froggy does everything he can think of to avoid going to bed. An amusingly illustrated book.

Keeping safe

Burningham, J. (1992) *Come Away from the Water, Shirley,* Cape, London
While Shirley's parents sit on the beach with their knitting and newspapers, Shirley embarks on a fantasy adventure, interrupted only when her parents become over-fussy.

Burningham, J. (1992) *The Shopping Basket,* Red Fox, London
An ordinary trip to the shop becomes an extraordinary adventure for Steven as he encounters all sorts of hazards on his way home and has to use his wits to overcome them.

Blake, Q. (1999) Mrs *Armitage, Queen of the Road,* Red Fox, London
Mrs Armitage arrives on the beach with her surfboard and her dog. She paddles out to sea to wait for the Big Wave. But Mrs Armitage can't be satisfied with just an ordinary surfboard and she is soon adding a hilarious variety of gadgets and contraptions. And when the Big Wave finally arrives, Mrs Armitage certainly surfs with style.

Clarke, J. (2007) *Dippy's Sleepover*, Red Fox, London
Dippy is really excited when he's invited to sleep at Spike Triceratops' house on Friday. They'll watch *Scarysaurs Go Wild* and eat popcorn and ... but there's one problem – Dippy wets the bed. Can he be dry by Friday?

Alborough, J. (1994) *Where's My Teddy?* Walker, London
Eddy has lost his teddy so he goes off into a dark wood to find him. At the same time a giant has lost his teddy. A charming tale to illustrate that even the biggest people can be afraid of something.

Cooper, H. (1994) *The Bear Under the Stairs*, Corgi, London
Only William thinks there is a bear who lives under the stairs. William imagines that the bear likes to eat little boys so he feeds the bear with scraps of food ...

McPhail, D. (1991) *Lost*, Little, Brown
What would you do if you came across a brown bear lost in a big city?

Self-esteem

Hoffman, M. (1991) *Amazing Grace*, Frances Lincoln, London
Grace learns that she can do anything if she wants to do it enough.

Clark, E.C. (1998) *I Love You Blue Kangaroo*, Andersen, London
A book about love and caring.

Oram, H. (1999) *Badger's Bad Mood*, Picture Lions, London
The best of us have bad moods but they can affect everyone around us.

Richardson, J. (2002) *Grunt*, Hutchinson, London
This little pig feels so different from his brothers and sisters that he runs away from home but on the way he learns an important lesson about being special.

Rogers, P. (2003) *Tiny*, Bodley Head, London
Tiny, the flea, lives on a very big dog called Cleopatra and learns that it isn't how big you are that matters, but how big you feel.

Loss, grief and separation

Burningham, J (1988) *Granpa*, Puffin Books, London
When Granpa dies a little girl is left with wonderful memories of a very special friendship.

Dupasquier, P. (2002) *Dear Daddy*, Anderson Press, London
Sophie writes to her father who is away at sea. What she says in her letters is illustrated and above these pictures are others showing what Daddy is doing. Eventually Daddy comes home and on the last page they are reunited.

Durant, A., (2003) *Always and Forever*, Doubleday, London
When Fox dies his friends think they will never get over their sadness, but when Squirrel calls she reminds them of all the funny things Fox did and they realise that Fox is still in their hearts and memories and will be with them forever.

Robinson, C. (1994) *Leaving Mrs Ellis*, Red Fox, London
A story about Leo who will be moving on to a new class and the loss he feels in leaving behind a loving teacher.

Selway, M. (1993) *Don't Forget to Write*, Red Fox, London
Rosie is going to stay with Grandad and Aunty Mabel and doesn't want to go. She writes letters to her family which start off with her wanting to come home immediately – and end up with her wanting to stay a little longer.

Simonds, P. (1989) *Fred*, Penguin, Harmondsworth
Lazy old Fred was just an ordinary cat, until he died and had the funeral of the century. A light-hearted story of the death and funeral of Fred, the superstar cat.

Varley, S. (1992) *Badger's Parting Gifts*, Julia McRae, London
When Badger dies, all his animal friends find it hard not to be sad, until they all realise they have a special memory of Badger. He had given each of them a parting gift that will help them too remember him forever.

Waddell, M. (1990) *Grandma's Bill*, Simon & Schuster, London
Bill didn't know he had a grandpa until he saw a photo when he visited Grandma. Grandma explained that he too had been called Bill and brought out the photo album

and shared all her memories with young Bill. Bill and Grandma look together at the pictures of the past and the present, sharing the reassuring sense of continuity.

Waddell, M. (1991) *Once There Were Giants*, Walker Books, London
A lovely story about the circle of life – baby growing up, moving on, leaving home and a new baby.

Wilhelm, H. (1985) *I'll Always Love You*, Hodder & Stoughton, London
A story of the close relationship between a boy and his dog and how he comes to terms with its death. Effie the dog grew quickly, got old, became ill and died. The boy's grief is tempered with the knowledge that he had repeatedly told his dog 'I'll always love you'.

Songbooks to enhance Circle Time

These songbooks contain songs that will provide interesting, fun ways to end the Circle Time sessions.

Apusskidu – 56 songs for children, A. & C. Black, London, 1975.

Bingo Lingo supporting language development with songs and rhymes, A. & C. Black, London, 1999.

Bobby Shafto Clap Your Hands by Sue Nicholls, A. & C. Black, London, 1992.

Count Me In – 44 songs and rhymes about numbers, A. & C. Black, London, 1984.

Game Songs by Harriet Powell, A. & C. Black, London, 1983.

Harlequin – 44 songs round the year, A. & C. Black, London, 1981.

High Low Dolly Pepper by Veronica Clark, A. & C. Black, London, 1991.

Jim along Josie by Nancy and John Langstaff, OUP, London, 1970.

Okki Tokki Unga – action songs for children, A. & C. Black, London, 1978.

Primrose Early Years Pack by Barbara Lipscomb, Primrose Publications Ltd, Lancaster, 1995.

Tinderbox – 66 songs for children, A. & C. Black, London, 1987.

Other books on Circle Time

Collins, M. (2003) *Enhancing Circle Time for the Very Young*, Paul Chapman Publishing, London.

Collins, M. (2004) *Circling Safely*, Paul Chapman Publishing, London.

Collins, M. (2005) It's *OK to be Sad*, Paul Chapman Publishing, London.

Collins, M. (2006) *Music and Circle Time*, Paul Chapman Publishing, London.